THE WORLD'S MOST EVIL PSYCHOPATHS

THE WORLD'S MOST EVIL PSYCHOPATHS

HORRIFYING TRUE-LIFE CASES

JOHN MARLOWE

ARCTURUS

ARCTURUS

This edition published in 2016 by Arcturus Publishing Limited
26/27 Bickels Yard, 151–153 Bermondsey Street,
London SE1 3HA

ISBN: 978-1-78428-557-9
AD000485UK

Printed in China

CONTENTS

INTRODUCTION

One hundred years ago, a book on the subject of psychopaths would most certainly have included very different cases from some of the ones contained between these covers. At that time, when the crimes of Jack the Ripper and Joseph Vacher were still well within living memory, the word 'psychopath' would have been used to denote any form of mental illness. But in describing someone as a psychopath today, we are more often than not referring to a person who has no concern for the feelings of others, an individual lacking any sense of social obligation.

Of course, very few psychopaths ever commit murder. The individuals included here are remembered because the extent of their cruelty set them apart from the rest of humanity. These are people who took delight in inflicting pain and death on others. All might be considered serial killers or spree killers, though most committed their crimes well before either term came into common use.

The earliest examples in this book are members of the nobility. Holding great wealth and political power, they perpetrated their misdeeds before police departments and other law enforcement bodies ever existed. Historical figures such as Gilles de Rais and Elizabeth Báthory committed their crimes with at least the partial knowledge of fellow members of the aristocracy.

We know of their activities today through court documents. Vlad III Draculea, on the other hand, has become a legendary figure through oral history, a record given to exaggeration and fancy. And yet, despite an absence of documentary evidence, we are virtually certain that this prince of Wallachia is guilty of having committed inhuman acts.

The same cannot be said about Sweeney Todd, the Demon Barber of Fleet Street, whose very existence, never mind crimes, has been debated for generations. In all likelihood, Sweeney Todd is nothing more than one more creation of the fertile imagination of Thomas Prest, a 19th-century contributor to the penny dreadfuls.

It is in Prest's 1846 story, 'The String of Pearls: A Romance', that the barber's name first sees print. No one has yet uncovered files relating to *Rex v Sweeney Todd*, the trial that is said to have sent this 18th-century serial killer to the gallows.

The most that one can usually say in support of Mr Todd's existence is that Prest's writing was often inspired by actual crimes.

Thomas Prest's method continues to be used today. Author Thomas Harris, who was in the courtroom for portions of Ted Bundy's 1979 murder trial, later incorporated the serial killer's techniques in creating the character James 'Buffalo Bill' Gumb in *The Silence of the Lambs*. The long history of murders committed by the Monster of Florence inspired Harris to set the 1999 sequel, *Hannibal*, in the Italian city.

Those studying American literature may one day be introduced to Jeffrey Dahmer through the character he inspired: Quentin P., the protagonist of Joyce Carol Oates' award-winning 1995 novel, *Zombie*. Other murderers found their stories adapted for the silver screen. John Wayne Gacy, 'the Killer Clown', lived long enough to see himself portrayed by the Tony award-winning actor Brian Dennehy in 1992's *To Catch a Killer*.

Of course, no killer has found his way into fiction and film more often than Jack the Ripper. He features in the novels of such varied writers as William S. Burroughs, Philip José Farmer and Colin Wilson, among many others, and has had a hold on the public's imagination like no other before or since. This can at least partly be explained by the fact that he was never caught. He remains a shadow, one might say a phantom.

In Nicholas Meyer's 1979 film *Time After Time*, Jack the Ripper steals H. G. Wells' famous time machine and is transported into the 20th century. After witnessing the destruction and death surrounding him, he says, 'Ninety years ago I was a freak. Today I'm an amateur.'

Omar Mateen, who murdered 49 people at Pulse nightclub in Orlando, Florida

Indeed, the early part of the century saw war fought on a previously unimaginable scale. As if reflecting this, the frequency of psychopathic killing continued to rise. The body counts of serial killers such as Fritz Haarmann, Gary Ridgway and Andrei Chikatilo are many times that of Saucy Jack.

As the century progressed, advances in the technology of firearms helped bring about the rise of the spree killer. Mass murderers were now able to kill with a speed and efficiency that would once have been unimaginable. In carrying out the Columbine High School massacre, on 20 April 1999, Eric Harris and Dylan Klebold used a 12-gauge

Savage-Springfield 67H pump-action shotgun, a Hi-Point 995 Carbine 9mm semi-automatic rifle, a 9mm Intratec Tec-9 semi-automatic handgun and a 12-gauge Stevens 311 D double-barrelled shotgun. Within 45 minutes, they had killed 12 students and a teacher, and had wounded 24 others. The slaughter only ended when they both committed suicide.

The murderers featured here rarely chose their equals as victims. Edmund Kemper – standing 6 foot, 9 inches – murdered women he towered over. Others, like Peter Kürten, Adam Lanza and spree killer Thomas Hamilton, counted children among their victims. Even Harris and Klebold, who went after their fellow high school students – as well as Omar Mateen in Orlando – had a very distinct advantage in the firearms they carried.

In this way, the serial killers and spree killers of our time have something in common with those of the nobility centuries ago. They seek to exercise power over who lives and who dies.

But our modern way of life provides a unique reward for killers who feel inferior and ignored, and who can raise the body count sufficiently to make the news headlines. As one of them boasted in a manifesto of murder published on the internet, 'I have noticed that so many people [that kill] are all alone and unknown, yet when they spill a little blood the whole world knows who they are. A man who is known by no one is known by everyone, his name across the lips of every person on the planet, all in the course of one day. Seems the more people you kill, the more you're in the limelight.'

John Marlowe
Montreal

A BLOODY HISTORY

History records a lengthy procession of souls who have committed acts of unspeakable evil. At the very front are certain aristocrats. Abusing their positions of privilege and power, they were able to murder, rape and torture with impunity — but only for a time. They are historic figures who have become legends in their own cultures and, in some particularly gruesome cases, have come to be known throughout the world.

GILLES DE RAIS

A nobleman and soldier, Gilles de Rais fought beside Joan of Arc during the siege of Orléans; in fact, this saint of the Roman Catholic Church was one of his greatest supporters. However, he is not remembered for his heroism or his accomplishments on the field of battle. Rais holds a place in history as one of the earliest recorded serial killers.

Nobleman Gilles de Rais fought alongside Joan of Arc during the siege of Orléans

Gilles de Rais was born in the autumn of 1404 within the appropriately named Tour Noir at the château of Champtocé. His father, Guy de Montmorency-Laval, was one of the wealthiest men in France. Intelligent and shrewd, he had achieved his status through a number of legal and political manoeuvres, one of which was his marriage to Marie de Craon, Gilles' mother. After both parents died – his father suffered a lengthy demise after having been gored by a wild boar – Gilles inherited the barony in the Duchy of Rais (now Retz).

Gilles ended up under the tutelage of his grandfather, Jean de Craon, a man schooled in the arts of manipulation and thievery. After two failed endeavours to marry his grandson into other powerful French houses, Jean became determined that Gilles would wed his cousin, Catherine de Thouars. He accomplished this union by directing the 16-year-old Gilles to abduct his bride. There was an attempt at liberation, but Catherine's would-be rescuers were thrown into the dungeon at Champtocé and the marriage took place as planned.

In 1427, Gilles was made a commander in the royal army, supporting Charles VII in his efforts to gain the disputed French crown. He fought alongside Joan of Arc in several military campaigns and on 17 July 1429 was honoured at the coronation of Charles VII at Reims.

That particular ceremony, which he had helped prepare by carrying Charles' anointing oil from Paris, marked the pinnacle of Gilles' stature. A series of political and military blunders followed the coronation. Joan was captured the following year, and on 31 May 1431 was famously burned at the stake. In November 1432, Gilles' grandfather died. On his deathbed, Jean de Craon repented his various misdeeds. The wealthy old man dispensed his money and property, compensated those from whom he'd stolen, and provided endowments to two hospitals. Gilles received nothing.

With the death of his former mentor, Rais was left alone to navigate the rather difficult waters of French politics. Lacking the talent and cunning of his father and grandfather, he saw his power and influence quickly evaporate. Worsening matters was the fact that he had been experiencing financial difficulties, and in the months leading up to his grandfather's death had begun selling off parcels of the old man's land.

It appeared as if every venture was ill-considered and foolish. Among the greatest of his miscalculations was the 1435 staging of *Le Mistère du Siège d'Orléans*. Intended to celebrate the tenth anniversary of the triumph he had shared with Joan of Arc, it was a lavish production requiring a cast of over 600. In the end, it was this same ineptitude, his inability to perform the intricate legal and political manoeuvres required of the nobility, which set in motion the events leading to his downfall and, ultimately, death.

One of the many properties with which Rais had been forced to part was a château in the village of Sainte-Etienne-de-Mar-Morte. The purchaser, Geoffrey le Ferron, entrusted the property to his brother Jean, a Roman Catholic priest. However, Rais was never happy with the decision he'd made, and in 1440, two years after the sale, the baron chose to forcibly take back his former estate. On 15 May, Rais led a band of 70 men to Sainte-Etienne, burst into the village church, kidnapped Jean le Ferron and seized the château. When news of the abduction and violation of ecclesiastical property reached the Bishop of Nantes, an investigation was launched. What he discovered was that the abduction and violation were very much the least of Rais' crimes.

As Gilles was in the favour of Charles VII, those charged with bringing the nobleman to justice moved slowly and with caution. In August, troops of the royal army marched against one of Rais' castles, freeing the priest, Jean le Ferron. Three weeks later, Rais and four members of his circle were placed under arrest on charges that included murder, sodomy and heresy.

On 21 October, Gilles confessed his crimes. Testimony at his trial revealed a horror that stretched back seven years, to the months following the death of Jean de Craon. It was at this point that Gilles, a man who had previously killed only in battle, had turned to murder. His first victim is said to have been a boy named Jean Jeudon, who was kidnapped and brought to

Abductions led to murder for Gilles de Rais: he once sodomized a boy dangling on a hook, then killed him

Illustration of de Rais disposing of a woman's corpse, from Histoire de la Prostitution at de la Débauche Chez Tous les Peuples du Globe *(1879)*

Gilles' castle at Machecoul. There, before the nobleman's intimate circle, he was sodomized twice by Gilles – once while dangling at the end of a hook. The child was then killed.

Other children, most often young boys, were either abducted or lured to Gilles' various residences. They were sexually assaulted, tortured and mutilated. According to testimony, the baron and his circle would set up the severed heads of the children in order to judge which was the most attractive victim. The testimony was said to be so horrific that the worst portions were ordered to be stricken from the record.

The only explanation offered for Gilles' actions was that he had begun to experiment with the occult. An attractive young man named Francesco Prelati, who had been schooled in the fields of alchemy and evocation, had promised the nobleman that he would regain his lost fortune by sacrificing children to a demon known as 'Barron'.

The precise number of Rais' victims is not known. Most of the bodies were dismembered and burned or buried. Although the fates of 37 victims were discussed at trial, the true number is likely to be much higher. Two days after the baron's confession, the court sentenced him to death. He was then excommunicated by the ecclesiastical court. After a dramatic expression of remorse by Gilles, the Church rescinded its punishment. On 26 October, Gilles went to his execution pleading with his friends to pray that their souls too might be saved. His corpse was thrown on a pyre, only to be rescued by the very bishop who had instigated the damning investigation. Rais was buried with Catholic rites.

VLAD III

Vlad III Draculea was known in his day as Vlad the Impaler. The origins of this epithet most probably lie with the Turks, who came to call him *Kaziglu Bey* – 'the Prince Impaler'. It is a reference to his preferred method of execution. Most often a sharpened stake was inserted in a victim's anus and forced through the body until it came out of the mouth. Stakes might be pushed through other orifices. Infants were said to be impaled on a stake driven through their mothers' breasts.

He was born late in the year 1431, probably in the Transylvanian fortress city of Sighisoara. His father was Vlad II Dracul, a Romanian surname which can be translated as 'Dragon'. Thus, Vlad III was Draculea, 'Son of the Dragon'. Five years after his birth, Vlad III became Prince of Wallachia, in present-day Romania.

When Vlad was ten, his father sent him and his younger brother Radu the Handsome as hostages to the Ottoman sultan Murad II. He spent much of the next six years locked in an underground dungeon in Turkey where he was whipped and beaten. Radu, on the other hand, became a favourite of the sultan's son. He lived a life of comfort and became a convert to Islam.

Even during the Middle Ages, the torture methods of Vlad III stood out as particularly brutal and sadistic

Vlad's return to Wallachia was made possible only through the murder of his older brother, Mircea, who was buried alive after having been blinded by hot iron stakes, and the subsequent assassination of his father. Murad II then installed Vlad III as a puppet prince. Mere months later, Vlad was pushed out of Wallachia by troops loyal to the kingdom of Hungary. He fled to Moldavia, where he was put under the protection of his uncle. After his uncle, too, was assassinated, Vlad switched his allegiance from the Ottoman empire to the kingdom of Hungary. In 1456, he led a successful campaign sweeping the Turks out of Wallachia, and was again installed as prince. The next six years were spent in an effort to consolidate his power. This Vlad achieved through a variety of means, not the least of which were torture and murder.

Clapped in irons

In 1462, he lost Wallachia when troops of the Ottoman empire again invaded. His wife, whose name is left unrecorded, committed suicide for fear of being captured. Vlad's brother Radu became the new prince. Under an agreement struck between the Hungarian king and Sultan Mehmed II, ruler of the Ottoman empire, Vlad was imprisoned in Hungary. It is doubtful that his confinement lasted four years; in 1466, he married into the Hungarian royal family and was officially released from custody eight years later.

In 1475, he attempted to take back Wallachia. Radu was now dead, but he

Vlad the Impaler had unusual notions of hospitality: when he executed prisoners in his castle, his preferred method was to insert a sharpened stake in the anus and force it through the body until it came out of the mouth

had a new foe, Basarb the Elder, with whom to contend. It was an easy victory, but afterwards the troops that had helped to restore Vlad returned to Transylvania. He was left with a citizenry which he had once terrorized. When the Turks returned with reinforcements, Vlad was at their mercy.

Vlad III died in December 1476. Most accounts place him on the battlefield at the moment of death; facing defeat, surrounded by his men. One story has it that he was accidentally killed by one of his own as the battle's end drew near.

After his death, Vlad's corpse was decapitated, preserved in honey and sent to Istanbul where the head was displayed, appropriately, atop a stake. According to records, his body was buried at the monastery at Snagof, on an island close to Bucharest. However, recent excavations there have uncovered only some bones of horses. Dating from the Neolithic era, they do not at all correspond with what one would expect of a Wallachian prince.

It is an indication of the particularly brutal and sadistic nature of Vlad that his techniques of punishment and torture stand out in the Middle Ages. The earliest written record in which his atrocities are detailed is a German pamphlet issued in the Holy Roman Empire. Printed in 1488, 12 years after his death, it paints the late prince as a sadistic monster, forever terrorizing his people. Romanian oral tradition, however, appears divided. Some tales portray him as harsh but fair; a ruler who expected his people to be honest and moral. Only those who

Vlad inspired Bram Stoker's Dracula

deviated from this path were dealt with in a brutal manner. Other oral records depict a cruel man who delighted in torture and punishment. This Vlad was a prince who employed a variety of methods in torturing his victims, including skinning, boiling, scalping, decapitation, blinding, strangling, hanging, burning and frying. He was said to delight in cutting off various body parts – the nose, the ears, the genitals and the tongue – as punishment.

Oral tradition has it that these techniques were not used exclusively against the Turks, but also on his own people. In the years 1457, 1459 and 1460, he tortured and murdered tradesmen and merchants who dared rebel against his laws. It is said that in August 1459, he had impaled 30,000 merchants and administrators in the city of Brasov.

The Ottoman invasion of 1462 was caused, in part, by the reception he had given an emissary of the sultan. When the emissary was granted an audience with Vlad, he was told to remove his turban. After the order was ignored, the prince had the turban nailed to the man's head.

ELIZABETH BÁTHORY

Born to nobility, Elizabeth Báthory – Báthory Erzsébet – used her power and privilege to become the most infamous serial killer in Hungarian history. However, her most notorious crime, the one for which she is remembered today, is a fabrication promoted by an 18th-century monk.

The Countess Elizabeth Báthory was born on 7 August 1560 on her family's Nyírbátor estate in the Northern Great Plain region of eastern Hungary. Her father, George Báthory, held enormous wealth, exceeding that of the Hungarian king Matthias. Her mother, Anna Báthory, was the older sister of the Polish king Stephan. George was her third husband. In marrying, Elizabeth's parents had united two branches of a powerful family, and in doing so had carried forward the long tradition of interbreeding among the noble clans.

A woman of the Renaissance, Elizabeth spent her early years at Ecsed Castle, where she learned to read and write in four anguages. At the age of 11 years, she became engaged to Ferencz Nádasdy, the

Elizabeth Báthory fully shared her husband's torture-loving cruelty and sadistic impulses

son of another aristocratic Hungarian family, and moved to be with her future husband's family at Nádasdy Castle in the westernmost portion of the country. Such was the status of the Báthory family that upon their marriage, on 9 May 1575, the groom adopted the bride's name. This is not to say that the former Ferencz Nádasdy did not himself have considerable wealth. His wedding gift to Elizabeth was their home, Cachtice Castle, an expansive country house and 17 adjacent villages.

Although Ferencz Báthory was but one of countless men in history who have been dubbed 'the Black Knight', he was nevertheless notably cruel. Three years into the marriage, he was made the chief commander of the Hungarian soldiers against the Turks during the height of the Long War. He took particular pleasure in personally devising tortures for his Turkish prisoners, and is said to have taught torture techniques to his wife. It is thought that the countess not only shared her husband's sadistic impulses, but that her passion for such things far outstripped those of the Black Knight. In fact, it has been suggested that Ferencz Báthory, hardly a gentle man, put something of a restraint on his wife, ensuring that her inclinations remained tempered and discreet.

After the death of Ferencz in 1604 – likely due to illness, but often claimed as having been at the hands of a prostitute – Elizabeth displayed much less discretion. The number of her victims and the degree of her cruelty both grew at a dramatic rate.

Her earliest victims were often local peasant girls, who came to the castle under the impression that they were to begin relatively beneficial servitude as housemaids. Later, Elizabeth became so bold as to abuse the daughters of the lower gentry who had been entrusted to her for the purposes of learning etiquette.

As early as two years prior to the death of Ferencz Báthory, rumours and complaints about Elizabeth's various activities had begun to find their way to the court in Vienna, from which the Habsburgs ruled Hungary. Initially, these appear to have been brushed aside; but as the years passed – and Elizabeth began to abuse the daughters of the lower gentry – her conduct could be ignored no longer.

In March 1610 an inquiry was established. Evidence was so damning that negotiations were soon entered into with others in the Báthory family, including

Local servant girls arrived at the Báthory castle hoping that servitude would be relatively benign

Elizabeth's surviving son. It was decided that in order to avoid scandal and the disgrace of a noble and influential name, Elizabeth would receive no punishment. Rather she would be placed under house arrest and spend the remainder of her life at the castle.

On the morning of 29 December 1610, a group of men under the guidance of the Palatine of Hungary, George Thurzó, entered the castle. They discovered one girl recently deceased, two others who were mortally wounded, and a number of others who had been locked up. However, these were far from the most horrific sights. Elizabeth had disposed of her victims without care. Frequently, they were simply shoved under beds – if the stench became too great, servants were instructed to remove the bodies and leave them in the surrounding fields. Both whole corpses and body parts were found throughout the castle.

On 7 January 1611, four maids, considered Elizabeth's collaborators, were put on trial. Of these only one escaped execution. While the noble lady was sent to live out the rest of her days in a tower room, two of her maids had their fingers cut off and were thrown on a pyre; another servant was beheaded.

In rendering their verdict, a panel of 21 judges considered the testimonies that had been collected over the preceding ten months. It was claimed that Elizabeth had tortured and killed her victims not only at the castle, but on her other properties and during trips to Vienna. More often than not, the claims against Elizabeth were based on hearsay. Her crimes, though, were many. She would push needles under the finger and toe nails of her maids and place red-hot coins and keys on their hands, faces or genitalia. In winter, she would throw young girls into the snow and pour cold water over them, allowing her victims to freeze. Some girls would simply be left to starve to death. She was also said to take great delight in biting the flesh off faces and other parts of the body – always while her victim was still alive.

Exactly how many girls

Elizabeth Báthory corrupted her maidservants and had them collaborate with her in torture, mutilation and even murder

suffered death at the hands of Elizabeth is unknown. One witness mentioned a book written by Elizabeth, which was claimed to have contained the names of more than 650 of her victims. Although the book has not survived and the figure is not mentioned by any other witness, the death toll of 650 has remained, becoming an integral part of Elizabeth Báthory's legend. However, her collaborators put the number at less than 50, while others working in the castle gave estimates of between 100 and 200 girls.

After learning the extent and nature of Elizabeth's crimes, Mattias II, emperor of Hungary, encouraged Thurzó to put her on trial. Though reluctant to break the agreement with the Báthory family, he began to collect more evidence. It has been suggested that what Thurzó was actually doing was playing for time. If so, his ploy worked. Elizabeth lived under house arrest for less than four years. She was found by a servant, dead in her tower room on the evening of 21 August 1614.

IMAGINED ATROCITIES

As if Elizabeth Báthory's crimes weren't sufficiently repulsive, over time her story has been embellished by the addition of imagined atrocities. The most prevalent of these fabrications is the idea that the countess had virgins murdered in order to bathe in their blood. In doing so, the story goes, Elizabeth believed she could retain her youth and beauty. Although the source of this story has been lost to history, the first recorded account was written by a Jesuit scholar, László Turóczi, in his 1729 *Tragica Historia*. In the three centuries since, this invented atrocity has been pointed to as the ultimate in female vanity.

BURKE AND HARE

On 28 January 1829, the body of an executed prisoner, William Burke, was brought to the University of Edinburgh. It was studied and dissected under the eyes of medical students, professors and interested members of the public. The prisoner's skeleton was removed, cleaned and readied for display in the university's medical school. His skin was put to use in the crafting of a variety of items, including the binding of a small book that remains to this day on display in the Surgeons' Hall Museum, Royal College of Surgeons of Edinburgh. It was a fitting end to one of the most notorious murderers in Scottish history.

Born in 1792, within the parish of Urney, County Tyrone, Ireland, Burke had spent seven years in the militia, had married and fathered two children. In about 1817, he emigrated to Scotland. Though he would claim that he wrote to his wife frequently – letters that were unanswered – it is likely that he abandoned the family. In Scotland, Burke led something of a transient existence, working as a baker, a cobbler and a labourer. While working on the Union Canal, he met a woman who called herself Helen McDougal. This was not her legal name; years earlier she had separated from her husband, and had taken up with a sawyer whose name she had adopted. Together they had two children, who Helen summarily abandoned when she and Burke ran off on a journey that would eventually lead them to Edinburgh.

William Hare, too, had come to Scotland from Ireland. Like Burke, he had laboured on the Union Canal, where he befriended a man named Logue. In 1822, after the project was completed, Hare found work loading and unloading canal boats. He became a tenant in Logue's squalid seven-bed Edinburgh lodging house, but the stay was short-lived. The two friends had a falling-out, likely precipitated by the interest Hare was taking in Logue's wife, Margaret. When Logue died, in 1826, Hare returned to the house and, after a brief competition with a rival lodger, was soon living as the common-law husband of the widow.

By 1827, William Burke and Helen McDougal had established themselves as regular tenants in the lodging house run by William Hare and Margaret Logue. Though it would be incorrect to describe the two couples as friends, they were united by common interests – whisky and money – both of which, it seemed, they were forever lacking. This would change in November 1827, when a tenant

William Burke, who was executed in 1829, and William Hare: medical science was hungry for corpses and the two 'bodysnatchers' found a wicked way of supplying these as well as turning a nice little profit for themselves

Edinburgh's graveyards offered a ready supply of bodies to sell to the anatomists, but it was hard work digging at midnight and you might be caught in the act. Burke and Hare soon worked out a better way of acquiring corpses

known as Old Donald, an army pensioner, died of 'a dropsy' [bodily distemper] owing £4 rent. Annoyed by the debt, Hare enlisted Burke's help in stealing the body from its coffin, and replaced it with an equal weight of tanner's bark. A man familiar with the less respectable side of Edinburgh, Hare knew that Old Donald's body would be of some value to the city's schools of medicine. After dark, they recovered the body from its hiding place and carried it in a sack to an anatomy school at No. 10 Surgeons' Square. There it was received by three assistants of Dr Robert Knox, one of the foremost professors of anatomy in Scotland. For their troubles, Burke and Hare received £7 10s, nearly three pounds below market value. Still, it was a significant sum, and the pair were elated to have made such a gain with so little effort.

Not long after, another tenant, a miller named Joseph, developed a high fever and became delirious. Fearing news of Joseph's illness would affect business, Hare grew concerned, but it wasn't long before he'd turned the situation to his advantage. He summoned Burke to Joseph's bedside. There the pair determined that the miller was most certainly going to die of fever. They plied Joseph with drink, after which Burke suffocated the man with his pillow. That evening, they took the body to Dr Knox's lecture rooms.

The winter passed, and with it the £10 Burke and Hare had been given for the body of Joseph the miller. By February 1828, the pair were again looking to supplement their incomes through the good graces of Dr Knox. However, despite Edinburgh's dire problems with sanitation, and the miserable winter weather, all appeared healthy at the lodging house. The pair looked outside their door, figuring that no one was likely to miss those who considered the street their home. Their next victim was Abigail Simpson, an impoverished and elderly former employee of Sir John Hope, who had travelled by foot to Edinburgh in order to collect her pension – 18 pence and a can of broth. She was on her way back home when she met Hare, who invited her to the lodging house for a small drink. It is probable that Burke and Hare intended to kill Abigail that evening, but became too drunk to carry out the plan. She, too, was drunk, and ended up staying the night. Upon awakening the next morning she began a new round of drinking. Burke and Hare took pains to remain sober, and when Abigail fell asleep they smothered her.

That evening, the occasion of their third visit to No. 10 Surgeons' Square, the pair met Dr Knox for the first time. The professor was pleased with the corpse and authorized a payment of £10. As would become the routine, the profit was split three ways: £4 went to Burke, £5 went to Hare, and £1 was given to Margaret Logue as the owner of the lodging house that was proving so useful.

Over the next six months, Dr Knox would see a lot of Burke and Hare, as the pair murdered with greater frequency. They charitably put an end to the life of a tenant suffering from poor health. They suffocated an old woman Margaret had encountered in the street and had brought back to the lodging house. In April, Burke brought two teenaged prostitutes to his brother's modest home, one of whom he and Hare killed after the other had left the house. Afterwards, the two men dared to carry the body in a sack through the Edinburgh afternoon. A group of schoolboys taunted them, chanting 'They're carrying a corpse!' But they were not caught.

It seems that for the first time in their lives, Burke and Hare had money – and yet it wasn't enough. They drank more, and spent freely. This new-found wealth did not go unnoticed by their neighbours, to whom Burke, Hare and their common-law wives offered a variety of explanations, including Helen's rather improbable tale that her man served as a gigolo for a wealthy woman in the New Town.

The close call they had experienced in transporting the prostitute's corpse to Dr Knox did nothing to slow down the murderers. Indeed, it might be said that the pair had been emboldened by the experience. One morning, shortly after murdering a beggar-woman named Effie, whom Burke had known through his work as a cobbler, he encountered two policemen escorting a drunken woman they'd found in a stairwell. Boldly, he approached the two men and offered to take the woman to her lodgings. The offer was accepted and before the day was through, her corpse was lying in Dr Knox's lecture hall.

The next two victims were an elderly woman and her deaf grandson, after which Burke took a holiday, spending midsummer with Helen's relatives. Upon his return, he became suspicious that his partner had continued the lucrative business without him. An inquiry at Dr Knox's school revealed that Hare had indeed sold the body of a woman in his absence. Although Burke and Helen left the lodging house in anger, it wasn't long before the men resumed their trade.

The next victim was a Mrs Ostler, whom Burke lured into the lodging house during the celebration of a neighbour's newborn child. Mrs Ostler's murder was soon followed by

Sketch of Dr Knox, the physician who did not ask too many questions about where his corpses were coming from

that of Helen's cousin, Ann McDougal, whom Burke had met earlier that summer and had invited to visit the couple in Edinburgh. Next, Hare picked up an elderly prostitute named Mary Haldane. She was summarily murdered, followed by Peggy, her daughter, who had confronted Hare as to her mother's whereabouts.

The decision to murder Mary Haldane was yet another indication of the brazen attitude the two men had developed. Past victims had been loners, most often people whose disappearance would have gone unnoticed, but Mary Haldane had been a well-known character. Her sudden departure from the streets of Edinburgh was the subject of some talk. The fact that her daughter was also missing added greatly to the mystery.

Burke and Hare's next victim, a mentally handicapped young man named Jamie Wilson – Daft Jamie – was not only well-known, but well loved.

When his corpse was brought in to Dr Knox's lecture room, several students recognized it as Jamie. For his part, the professor denied that it was Daft Jamie laid out on the table, yet went to work immediately in dissecting the body laid out before him.

By Hallowe'en, 1828, Burke and Hare's luck had all but run out, but they would still manage one final murder. The victim was an Irish woman, Mary

Docherty, whom Burke invited to the lodging house by claiming some family connection. Her body was discovered the next evening by Ann Gray, one of Margaret's tenants. As Gray and her husband ran for the police, Burke and Hare disposed of the body through their usual method. They delivered the corpse to Dr Knox's premises, where it was discovered the next day by the authorities.

AVOIDING THE NOOSE

Burke, Hare, Helen and Margaret were all arrested. As the evidence was thought to be thin, Hare was offered immunity from prosecution so long as he testified against his business partner. His testimony led to Burke's death sentence. Helen, his common-law wife, was released – her complicity in the murders could not be proven. Returning to her home, she was almost lynched by an angry mob. She is thought to have fled first to England, then to Australia. Margaret, too, escaped the noose and was rumoured to have settled in Ireland.

In February 1829, Hare was released. There are various stories concerning his fate – that he became a blind beggar on the streets of London, or that he was thrown into a lime pit – but nothing is certain.

Dr Knox remained silent about his dealings with Burke and Hare. For several years, he continued his teaching, seemingly unaffected by public suspicion. Gradually, however, the consequences of his association with Burke and Hare became apparent. His student numbers dwindled, he was twice rejected by the University of Edinburgh and a brief stint at the Argyle Square Medical School proved not to be a success. He relocated to nearby Glasgow, then London, where he obtained a secure position with the Cancer Hospital.

Dr Knox died in 1862. During the last decade of his life, however, he achieved a certain degree of success as the author of *Fish and Fishing in the Lone Glens of Scotland* and *A Manual of Artistic Anatomy*, which he described as being 'for the use of sculptors, painters, and amateurs'.

EXECUTION of WILLIAM BURKE,
taken on the spot.

Published by Thomas Ireland Jan.r Edinburgh.

Edinburgh's citizens queued up to witness Burke's demise

VICTORIAN NIGHTMARES

The reign of Queen Victoria saw great advances in science and policing which enabled the detection of crimes that would have gone unnoticed at one time. Improvements in printing, combined with the advent of the telegraph and stenography, ensured that news was captured and spread at a previously unimaginable speed. The popular press was in its ascendancy and used much of its power to bring lurid stories of murder and sadism to the masses.

MARY ANN COTTON

Mary Ann Cotton was the most prolific serial killer in Victorian England. Among her victims were her mother, a lover, a friend, three husbands and numerous stepchildren. It is thought that she killed ten of her own children.

Her life began in Dickensian surroundings. She was born Mary Ann Robson, in October 1832, within Low Moorsley, a small village located not far from the city of Sunderland in north-east England. Consisting of herself, two younger siblings and Mary Ann's parents, the Robson family was not a large one. However, her father, a miner, seems to have been forever struggling to make ends meet. His life above ground was devoted to his two beliefs: Methodism and the idea that children must be raised with a firm hand.

When Mary Ann was 8, her father moved the family to nearby Murton, where he was employed by the South Hetton Coal Company. Any advancement the family had hoped to make through the relocation soon vanished after he fell 45 metres to his death down a mine shaft.

Six years later in 1846 Mary Ann's mother remarried. Although her stepfather had none of the financial worries that had plagued her father, the two men had at least one thing in common: the belief in strict discipline. At 16, Mary Ann escaped the family home by obtaining a position as a private nurse. She returned to her mother and stepfather three years later, but only for a brief period. Within months, a pregnant Mary Ann married William Mowbray, a labourer, and left the family home for good.

Mary Ann Cotton's father was a miner. His life above ground was devoted to two belief systems: Methodism [a meeting is pictured above] and the conviction that children must be raised with a firm hand

The young couple lived a somewhat transient lifestyle as Mowbray pursued work in the mines and in railway construction. Ultimately, they ended up where they had begun; in Sunderland, where Mowbray found work first as a foreman with the South Hetton Coal Company, then as a fireman aboard the steamer *Newburn*. In January 1865, Mowbray died of what was described as an intestinal disorder. Mary Ann received an insurance payment of £35 on his life. Wishing to express his condolences, the attending doctor revisited the house, surprising the widow who was dancing around the room in an expensive new dress.

During their 13-year marriage, Mary Ann and William Mowbray had had nine children, only two of whom were still alive when their father died.

After Mowbray's death, Mary Ann moved eight kilometres south to Seaham Harbour. She began a relationship with Joseph Nattrass, a man who was engaged to another woman. It was at this point that one of her two remaining children, a 3-year-old girl, died. After Nattrass married, Mary Ann returned to Sunderland with Isabella, her only surviving child. The girl was sent to live with her grandmother, and Mary Ann found employment with the Sunderland Infirmary House of Recovery for the Cure of Contagious Fever, Dispensary and Humane Society. While working there, she met an engineer named George Ward, who was suffering from a fever. His recovery was swift. Ward was discharged and, in August 1865, the two married. However, his ill-health returned soon after the wedding. During much of the marriage, he suffered from a lingering illness. Symptoms included paralyses and chronic stomach problems. When Ward died in October 1866, Mary Ann accused her late husband's doctor of malpractice.

As she had immediately after the death of her first husband, Mary Ann again left Sunderland. She settled in Pallion, where she was hired by a man named James Robinson. A shipwright, Robinson had also recently lost a spouse, and was in need of a housekeeper to look after his five children. But in December 1866, tragedy again struck the Robinson household when the youngest child died suddenly of gastric fever. Meanwhile Mary Ann, it seems, provided something more than sympathy for her new employer – she was soon with child.

Early in the New Year, Mary Ann received news that her mother had been taken ill. She made the trek back to Sunderland, arriving to find that her mother had all but recovered her health. Yet nine days later, she was dead.

With Isabella in tow, Mary Ann returned to her employer. Soon after their arrival, the girl began complaining of stomach pains, as did two of the Robinson children. By the end of April, all three were dead.

It can be said with some certainty that Robinson initially made no connection between the rash of deaths and his new housekeeper, for in August 1867 the two were married. The child Mary Ann was carrying, a daughter they named

Mary Ann Cotton became housekeeper to a shipwright called Robinson who needed someone to look after his five children

Mary Isabella, was born in late November. She lived for only three months.

The death of Mary Isabella proved to be the saddest event in a disastrous marriage. Although the couple would have one more child, the relationship deteriorated rapidly. Robinson soon came to the realization that his wife was running up debts without his knowledge and had stolen money he had asked her to deposit in the bank. After valuables began disappearing from the house, he confronted his children and was told that their stepmother had forced them to pawn the items. In late 1869, two years after they'd married, Mary Ann's husband threw her out of the house.

By the beginning of 1870, Mary Ann had been reduced to living on the streets. Her luck began to change when a friend, Margaret Cotton, introduced Mary Ann to her brother, Frederick. As in the case of Robinson, Frederick Cotton had been recently widowed. He'd also suffered through the deaths of two of his four children. Within a few months of meeting Mary Ann, he buried another child, who died of an apparent stomach ailment. Not long into the grieving process, Mary Ann became pregnant with Cotton's child. Early in the pregnancy, Margaret Cotton died of an ailment similar to that which had taken the life of her young nephew. Although Mary Ann was still married to Robinson – a secret she kept from the expectant father – she and Cotton were married in September 1870.

Shortly after the birth of her 11th child, a boy named Robert, Mary Ann heard news of Joseph Nattrass, her former lover. No longer married, Nattrass was living in the village of West Aukland, a little over 60 kilometres to the south. Not only did Mary Ann quickly move to resume the relationship, she somehow succeeded in convincing her husband to relocate the family closer to where Nattrass lived. Two days after his first wedding anniversary, Cotton died from a gastric fever.

Shortly after her husband's death, Mary Ann welcomed Nattrass into her home as a 'lodger'. Although she had received a substantial payment owing from Cotton's life insurance policy, she went to work as a nurse for John Quick-Manning, an excise officer who was recovering from smallpox. She soon became pregnant by him.

Between 10 March and 1 April, death visited the Cotton home on three separate occasions. The first to die was Frederick Cotton, Jr. His death was followed by Robert, the child of Mary Ann and her late husband. Before the infant could be buried, Joseph Nattrass also died; but only after rewriting his will so that all would be left to Mary Ann.

Once again pregnant, this time with Quick-Manning's child, Mary Ann's thoughts turned to marriage. It would appear that to her thinking only one obstacle remained: Charles, the surviving Cotton child. Mary Ann had hoped that he might be sent to a workhouse, but was told by Thomas Riley, a minor parish official, that she would be obliged to accompany him.

After declining, she informed Riley that Charles was sickly, adding, 'I won't be troubled long. He'll go like all the rest of the Cottons.' Riley, who had always seen the boy healthy, thought the statement peculiar. When Charles Cotton died five days later, he visited the village authorities and urged an investigation.

An inquest held the following Saturday determined that Charles had, indeed, died of natural causes. Mary Ann's story that Riley had made the accusation because she had spurned his advances would very likely have affected his position as well as his reputation, had it not been for the local press.

Reporters looking into Mary Ann's story discovered that she had buried three husbands, a prospective sister-in-law, a paramour, her mother and no fewer than 12 children, nearly all of whom had died of stomach ailments. The revelations caused the doctor who had attended Charles to reopen his

Mary Ann Cotton buried three husbands, a prospective sister-in-law, a 'paramour', her mother and no fewer than 12 children

investigation. He soon discovered traces of arsenic in the small samples he'd kept from the boy's stomach.

Mary Ann was arrested, and the body of Charles Cotton was exhumed. After another six corpses were dug up in failed attempts to locate the body of Joseph Nattrass, it was decided that she would stand trial for the murder of Charles alone. Proceedings were delayed a few months until the delivery of the baby fathered by Quick-Manning.

During the trial, Mary Ann attempted to explain Charles' death by saying that he had inhaled arsenic contained in the dye of the wallpaper of the Cotton home. The theory was dismissed and she was sentenced to death.

On 24 March 1873, Mary Ann Cotton was hanged at Durham County Gaol. Her death was long and painful, the result of an elderly hangman having miscalculated the required drop.

THE BLOODY BENDERS

In Kansas, the Bender family is legendary, and as with all legends, it is difficult to determine the difference between truth and embellishment. However, one claim that can be made with some certainty is that they were the first known serial killers operating in the United States.

Late in 1870, the Bender men arrived in Osage Township in the south-eastern part of Kansas. Like nearly all settlers, they came from the east, but exactly where from has always been something of a mystery. The assumption is that they were German. The patriarch, a giant of a man named John Bender Sr, barely spoke – his vocabulary seemed to consist of little more than muttered curses. His son, John Jr, was easily the more sociable of the two. Though he spoke with a German accent, he was fluent in English and given to laughter.

The two spent the remainder of 1870 and nearly all of the following year preparing their land and constructing a cabin and a barn, several kilometres south of the town of Cherry Vale. In the autumn, they brought Ma Bender and her daughter Kate to the new homestead. They used large pieces of canvas to divide their cabin in half. The back became the family home, while the other half was set up as a general store and inn offering lodging to weary travellers who passed along the Osage Trail. It was a good location, providing a tempting if modest place to stop for many lone men travelling from the east to a new life in the west.

Over the months that followed, people started going missing from along the Osage Trail. In a time of erratic and unreliable mail service, the disappearances weren't noticed at first; it was only over time, when the names of the missing had begun to accumulate, that suspicions began to be aroused. In neighbouring communities, rumour and speculation began to circulate.

Among the missing was a well-known physician, William H. York, who had disappeared in March 1873 while travelling the 160-kilometre route from Fort Scott to Independence, Kansas. Not long after the doctor's disappearance, the township decided that all farms in the area would be searched for evidence. Three days later, a local farmer noticed the Bender livestock roaming, obviously in need of nourishment. Further investigation revealed that the inn had been abandoned; nearly all possessions had been removed. The cabin itself contained a foul stench that was later found to be emanating from a trapdoor in the floor, beneath which was a pool of clotted blood.

Excavation of the apple orchard next to the cabin revealed ten bodies, including that of York. The doctor had been bludgeoned from behind and had had his throat cut. Eight other victims had been killed in the same manner; the sole exception was an 18-month-old girl who appeared to have been buried alive beneath her father's naked corpse. Dismembered parts of other victims were also found buried on the property. It was impossible to tell with any certainty exactly how many people the Bloody Benders had claimed.

The Benders were never seen again. They appeared to simply vanish into the Kansas landscape, leaving questions that have been answered by little more than speculation and fancy.

Among the more likely of the stories concerns the Bender daughter. Remembered as a voluptuous beauty, Kate, it is claimed, was one of the reasons travellers found the inn such an attractive place to spend the night.

As settlers buried their loved ones, a hue and cry ensued as many went off in search of the Benders. They were nowhere to be found. All traces had disappeared in the vast Kansas landscape, leaving many unanswered questions

Some stories tell of her performing throughout the region as 'Professor Miss Kate Bender', a psychic medium. Others depict her as a spiritualist who would perform a seance during which the unlucky traveller would be struck on the head through the canvas curtain dividing the cabin.

In fact, the canvas that divided the cabin in two always plays a role in the Bender legend. Although no one saw the family in action and lived to tell about it, their routine is described without variation. First, the unsuspecting guest would be struck through the curtain. The victim would then be dragged into the other half of the cabin, where he would be stripped of clothing and valuables. In the final step, the unlucky traveller would be thrown down the trapdoor to the cellar, where his throat would be cut.

The legends concerning the Bender clan extend as far as their respective fates. Several posses were formed to pursue the murderous family, including one that numbered among its members Charles Ingalls, father of *Little House on the Prairie* author Laura Ingalls Wilder. In her memoirs, Wilder writes of her belief that her father's posse caught the Benders and dealt with them in a manner typical of the American frontier. A number of different posses claimed that they had brought the Benders to justice, leaving open the intriguing possibility that several innocent people were killed by what amounted to little more than lynch mobs.

DEAD BABIES

It has been said that John Bender Sr ran off with all the money stolen from the victims, leaving the rest of the family penniless. One version of the legend has it that he committed suicide in Lake Michigan shortly after having been confronted by Ma and Kate.

A particularly gruesome story asserts that Kate and John Jr were not sister and brother; rather that they were lovers. According to this version of the Bender legend, the two had many babies together, each of which they disposed of with a hammer to the head. These killings presumably gave the couple practice for future dealings with those travelling the Osage Trail. It has been said that they fled first by train, then by horse into either Texas or Mexico, where John Jr died of a haemorrhage.

In his 1913 book *The Benders of Kansas*, Minnesota defence attorney John Towner James maintains that in 1889 Ma and Kate were captured in Michigan and brought to Kansas. According to James, the two women were to be tried for York's murder, but were let go when the trial date was postponed from February 1890 to May 1890. The story here is that the county didn't want the expense of lodging the prisoners for an three extra months.

As would be expected of a story in which imagination has replaced fact, the land once occupied by the Benders is said to be haunted by the ghosts of their victims.

THE SERVANT GIRL ANNIHILATOR

The American writer O. Henry is perhaps best remembered today for 'The Gift of the Magi', a Christmas tale featuring Jim and Della, a young couple with no money. As the holiday approaches, Della sells her long tresses to a wigmaker so that she might buy a platinum chain for Jim's watch. Meanwhile, Jim sells his watch and uses the money he receives to buy a set of jewelled combs for Della's hair. The moral is difficult to miss: material possessions, whether bejewelled or made from platinum, are of little value when compared to love. It is a heart-warming, sentimental story, typical of the author's work. How odd, then, that this very same man has the distinction of having provided a nickname for one of the first American serial killers, the Servant Girl Annihilator.

O. Henry's epithet, provided to friends working at the *Austin Daily Statesman*, was one of several used to describe the murderer who terrorized Texas between 1884 and 1885. Another name was the Austin Axe Murderer. Neither was entirely apt, but both continue to be used to this day for a killer who was never caught.

The Servant Girl Annihilator began his bloody work on the cold New Year's Eve of 1884. His first victim, a 25-year-old live-in 'negro servant' named Mollie Smith, was found next to the outhouse of the home in which she was employed. Wearing only a nightdress, she had been raped and bludgeoned to death. The murder weapon, an axe covered in Mollie's blood, was discovered inside the outhouse. No one in the house proper had heard anything. Indeed, all had appeared peaceful until Walter Spencer, Smith's common-law husband, had awoken from his usual night's sleep in great pain. He discovered a deep cut across his face. The bedroom he and Mollie shared was in bloody disarray and his 'wife' was gone. Spencer's cries for help awoke the rest of the house.

In the early morning hours, the local marshal led a pack of bloodhounds through the snow-covered streets of Austin. It was a horrible way to usher in the New Year.

Though Austin was then a small city – fewer than 25,000 lived within its limits – murder was not entirely unknown there. Still, the savagery displayed in Mollie Smith's death was big news indeed. Suspicion settled quickly on Smith's former lover, a black man named William Brooks. An all-white coroner's jury ignored Brooks' alibi and witnesses, concluding that he was probably guilty of the crime. Eventually, the ex-boyfriend was released due to lack of evidence.

Five months later, on 6 May, another black woman, Eliza Shelley, was murdered. A 30-year-old cook, Shelley lived with her three children in a cabin on the property of her employer, L. B. Johnson. It was Johnson's wife who, hearing Shelley's screams, sent her niece to check on the children. The girl found

There can be little doubt that in the midst of all this horror, some residents of Austin took comfort in the knowledge that all the Annihilator's victims had been black and were either servants or their close relatives

the family cook lying dead on the cabin floor, her skull very nearly split in two. Shelley's nightgown was raised, exposing most of her body. Bloody footprints of a barefooted man trailed from the awful scene.

This time, there had been a witness. The victim's 8-year-old son spoke of seeing a man enter the cabin. This unknown figure pushed the boy away and threw a blanket over him. Falling asleep, he'd seen nothing further, and had even slept through his mother's screams. Upon waking the next morning, he was blissfully unaware of her fate.

FALSE LEADS

Again, the authorities cast around for suspects. A mentally handicapped 19-year-old was arrested, seemingly for no other reason than that he had no shoes. When his feet were measured and shown to be of a different size to those of the killer, he was released. An acquaintance of the Shelleys was also held, for no other reason than that the two had been seen arguing.

The murderer struck again 17 days later. The victim, Irene Cross, was yet another black female servant. This time, it seemed, there had been no axe; it appeared that she had been stabbed in the head. One arm was almost severed from the rest of her body. In this case, the authorities arrested no one.

In August, the murderer entered the cottage of Rebecca Ramey, just one block south of where Eliza Shelley had been murdered three months earlier.

Approaching her bed, he knocked her out, and then abducted her daughter Mary. The 11-year-old was taken outside, raped and murdered. Again, there was no axe; the girl was stabbed through both ears with an iron rod. When she regained consciousness, Rebecca Ramey, a black servant of a man named Valentine Weed, remembered nothing of use.

The following month, the killer gained entrance to a servants' cabin behind the house of Major W. D. Dunham by climbing through a window. Stories about the night in question are varied and confused, but all agree that the first to be attacked was a man named Orange Washington, whose skull was caved in by a blow from an axe. Washington's common-law wife, Gracie Vance, was dragged out of the cabin and raped outside. Her friend, a visiting servant named Lucinda Boddy, received an axe blow to her head and was also raped.

The assaults ended when Major Dunham realized the noises were something much more than a domestic dispute, as he'd initially thought. Gun in hand, the major rushed outside, and the murderer fled. Gracie's body was found in the stables; her head had been beaten in with a brick. In one hand she clutched a gold watch, presumably torn from the killer during the struggle. Also present was an unidentified horse, saddled and tied. Both appeared to be excellent clues as to the identity of the assailant, and yet they proved to be of no use.

After detectives were brought in from Houston to assist in the investigation, two black men, Oliver Townsend and Dock Woods, were arrested. The evidence used against the two was less than compelling: a comment someone had overheard in which Townsend had told Woods he wanted to kill Gracie Vance.

In attempting to extract a confession from another suspect, a private detective agency resorted to torture and was discredited. Grasping at straws, the marshal arrested Walter Spencer, the

Black servants were on the lookout for an assailant who sought access to servant quarters, before raping and killing his victims

husband of Mollie Smith. His trial, based on the most improbable of theories, took just three days and resulted in an acquittal.

There can be little doubt that in the midst of all this horror, some residents of Austin took comfort in the knowledge that all the Annihilator's victims had been black and were either servants or their close relatives. All this changed on Christmas Eve when a middle-class white man, Moses Hancock, awoke to find that his wife, Sue, was missing. He soon found her lying behind their house. An axe had been used to split open her head, and a thin rod had been pushed into her brain. She had also been raped.

That same night, the body of another white woman, Eula Phillips, was found pinned under lumber in the alleyway of one of the city's wealthiest neighbourhoods. Her husband was found unconscious, having been hit on the back of the head with an axe.

The next day, hundreds of Austin residents left their Christmas festivities to attend an emergency meeting. A variety of initiatives – from increased lighting to early closure of taverns – were undertaken in the hopes of preventing further attacks. While the effect these moves had can be debated, the fact remains that the Servant Girl Annihilator never struck again.

Among the great mysteries surrounding the Annihilator is his change in victim type. What might have caused him to switch from poor, black female servants to comfortably-off white women? In 1885, some thought the answer obvious: Sue Hancock and Eula Phillips weren't victims of the Annihilator, but had been killed by their own husbands. Though it would appear unlikely that two men who did not know one another would think up the same idea and act on it during the same night, both were tried for the deaths of their wives. While Hancock was declared innocent, Phillips was found guilty of murder in the second degree. The verdict was later overturned by the Texas Court of Appeals for lack of evidence.

JACK THE RIPPER

His crimes have been investigated more than those of any other murderer. A whole field of study, Ripperology, is devoted to puzzling out his identity. And yet, 12 decades after his last murder, Jack the Ripper remains an elusive and mysterious figure.

Even the number and names of the victims have been the subject of considerable debate, though the majority of Ripperologists believe there to have been five victims, the first being Mary Ann Nichols. A 43-year-old alcoholic, she had much in common with the victims who would follow in her wake Nichols was estranged from her husband, and struggled to support herself through a variety of means. Indeed, at least four of the five women had been pushed further into poverty through the disintegration of their respective marriages. Nichols had been employed in workhouses, had worked as a domestic and had, on at least one occasion, resorted to stealing. She also tried to make ends meet as a prostitute, an occupation which, it seems, made her a target of the Ripper. Her body was discovered by two workmen in the early hours of 31 August 1888 on a back street not far from the London Hospital.

This portrayal of Jack the Ripper as a 'toff' in the film From Hell *may not come anywhere near the truth about who Jack the Ripper really was. It is now unlikely that anyone will ever prove beyond doubt who the killer was*

Nichols had had her throat cut. She had been stabbed repeatedly in the stomach and her abdomen had been cut open.

Eight days later, the Ripper claimed his second victim, a 47-year-old named Annie Chapman. Like Nichols, Chapman's throat had been slashed. Completely disembowelled, her intestines were thrown over one shoulder. Her uterus had been removed and was never found.

At approximately one o'clock on the morning of 30 September, the body of Elizabeth Stride, a 45-year-old Swedish immigrant, was found. She, too, had had her throat slit open. However, apart from an injury to her ear, Stride's body bore none of the butchery suffered by the previous victims. It is generally believed that the Ripper was interrupted before he could proceed any further.

Presumably dissatisfied with having had to leave his work on Stride's body unfinished, the Ripper struck again on the same evening. The second victim, 46-year-old Catherine Eddowes, had been picked up for public drunkenness the previous day by the Metropolitan Police. She was released at about the same time that Stride's body was discovered. Eddowes was last seen alive at approximately 1:30, talking to an unidentified man. Just 15 minutes later, her body was discovered. Working with great speed, the Ripper had cut her throat, sliced open her abdomen, thrown her intestines over her shoulder and removed her uterus and left kidney. He had also mutilated her face.

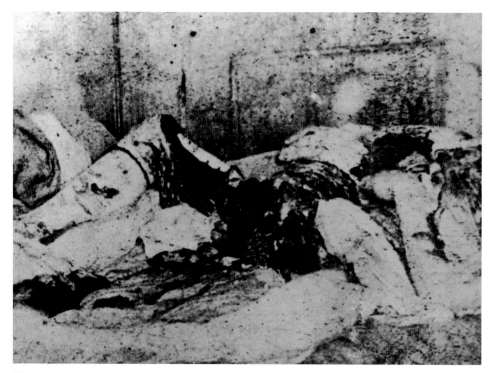

The body of Mary Kelly which was found in a sordid room at 13 Miller's Court in the East End of London. She was found naked on a bed – her throat had been slashed, her face mutilated and her abdomen sliced open

Following a period of inactivity, the final murder took place on 9 November. It is tempting to say that Mary Kelly was quite different from the other victims. She was, for example, at least two decades younger than the others. However, very little is known about Kelly and, as a result, many fanciful stories have been created about her life. In death, she stands apart from the others in that she was not killed in a public place, but in her own home. This gave the Ripper a great deal more time than he'd had with his previous victims, and it showed. Kelly's body was found naked, lying on her bed. The throat had been slashed and her face mutilated. The entire abdominal cavity had been emptied of its contents. Her breasts had been cut off – one had been placed under her head,

The Metropolitan Police left no stone unturned in their search for the Ripper, yet he led them a merry dance and gave them the slip

the other by her right foot. He liver was found between her feet. Some of the flesh removed from the abdomen and thighs had been placed on a table. Her heart was never found.

Though the number of victims claimed by Jack the Ripper pales when compared to those of Mary Ann Cotton, he has become a legend in a way she has not. While the butchery that accompanied his murders provides something of an explanation for this discrepancy, the role of the media cannot be ignored. Jack the Ripper killed at a time when inexpensive mass-circulation newspapers were in their ascendancy. News of the crimes spread rapidly through Great Britain and elsewhere. Some papers sought to exploit the crimes by reporting other murders as the work of Jack the Ripper. There is even a debate among Ripperologists as to the validity of the Jack the Ripper name, first used in a letter dated 25 September 1888, which was received by the Central News Agency. Some have argued that it was a hoax created to sell newspapers. Shortly after its publication, the Metropolitan Police were inundated with hundreds of letters bearing the epithet.

There were, of course, other factors which made the case of Jack the Ripper intriguing. His savagery appeared to escalate, reaching a crescendo with the murder of Mary Kelly. He appeared to have some education in surgery, most evident in his ability to eviscerate Catherine Eddowes in a matter of mere minutes. Above all, he was never caught, hence the speculation which continues to this day as to his identity.

Police officials at the time named six suspects as possibly being Jack the Ripper. The most interesting of these is Montague John Druitt. A barrister and assistant schoolmaster, Druitt committed suicide bydrowning shortly after the murder of Mary Kelly. Acoroner's jury concluded that he had been of unsound mind. Much of the contemporary interest in Druitt rests on statements that investigators had 'private information' which led some to conclude that he was the murderer.

Among the most cited suspects is Prince Albert Victor, grandson of Queen Victoria. One theory has it that the prince suffered from syphilis and was driven insane by the disease, but this is countered by royal records which show him to have been away from London on the dates when each of the murders were committed.

> Among the suspects is Prince Albert Victor. One theory has it that he suffered from syphilis and was driven insane by the disease

There are other theories which place the prince in a supporting role, most notably as the father of a child placed under the care of Mary Kelly. According to the most common version of this theory, Kelly was one of several women murdered by the physician Sir William Gull in an effort to suppress a scandal that would have jeopardized the future of the monarchy.

Some Ripperologists suspect Joseph Barnett, once the live-in lover of Mary Kelly, the Ripper's last victim. The thinking in this theory goes that Barnett committed the first four murders as a way of scaring Kelly into giving up prostituting herself to other men. When this proved ineffective, he flew into a rage and murdered his girlfriend. Thus, Barnett's link with Kelly would explain why the Ripper ceased killing after her murder.

Among the more fanciful theories is one claiming that Charles Dodgson, better known as Lewis Carroll, the author of *Alice's Adventures in Wonderland*, confessed his crimes through a series of anagrams found throughout his work…

JOSEPH VACHER

Joseph Vacher murdered and mutilated a total of 11 people, more than twice the number butchered by Jack the Ripper. Yet Vacher appears condemned to spend eternity standing in the shadow of his English contemporary. Even his nickname, the French Ripper, owes its existence to the Whitechapel killer and in his native France, he is known as '*Jack l'éventreur français*'.

Joseph Vacher explained his crimes by arguing that they were all the result of a crazed dog that had bitten him at the age of 8. His madness, he claimed, stemmed from rabies. Vacher added that medicine given to him by the village herbalist had had no effect other than to make him irritable and brutal, forever changing his character. Assuming Vacher's account of the dog to be true, it adds to a very small body of knowledge concerning the serial killer's childhood. We do know that he was born on 16 November 1869, in Isère, a department in the Rhône-Alpes region of France. He was the last of 15 children in a family of peasant farmers. His twin brother, the 14th in the family, choked to death when he was just one month old.

'The French Ripper':
Joseph Vacher
murdered and mutilated
11 people and put this
aberration down to the
fact that he was bitten by
a rabid dog at the age of
8. His twin brother choked
to death when he was one
month old

It is has been put forth that at 15 years of age Vacher may have committed his first murder. The victim, a 10-year-old boy, was raped and killed. In 1878, Vacher began studies with the Marist Brothers, but was returned home when it was discovered that he was having sexual relations with some of his fellow students. The following year, Vacher was convicted of having attempted to rape a young male farmhand. Whatever the sentence, it could not have been great – by that autumn he'd found employment as a server at a brewery in Grenoble. One account zsays that it was during this time that Vacher caught venereal disease from a prostitute. According to the story, the resulting infection forced the removal of a testicle.

> **For three years he drifted, begging and stealing to survive. He was also raping, murdering and mutilating men and women along his path**

It has also been claimed that he fell in with a group of anarchists. It is an unlikely association as in 1890, at the age of 21, Vacher enlisted in the French army. He was sent to the ancient city of Besançon, near the border with Switzerland. There he fell in love with a young servant girl, Louise Barrand, who considered him an object to be mocked.

Vacher the soldier developed a reputation as a brutal drillmaster. Although made a non-commissioned officer, he came to believe that his military service was not being properly recognized and, in both protest and desperation, attempted to slit his throat. Despite the suicide attempt, he remained with the army and was again promoted.

In June 1893, he proposed marriage to Louise. The offer was met with laughter and he attempted to kill the servant girl, but his gun misfired. Before he could be apprehended, he attempted suicide by shooting himself in the head. Although Vacher survived, the bullet remained lodged in his skull. The damage caused paralysis on the right side of his face; his right eye was also affected. It is also thought that Vacher did himself permanent brain damage, leading to headaches and overall mental instability.

Vacher was committed to an asylum in Dôle. There he was diagnosed as suffering from paranoia and hallucinations, and after six months, he was transferred to the Saint-Robert asylum in Isère. On April Fool's Day, 1894, he was considered cured and was discharged. Homeless and lacking the faculties required for work, Vacher wandered seemingly without aim throughout the countryside of south-eastern France.

Witnesses described him as a filthy, deformed figure; his injured eye seemed to be always discharging pus. Owing to the paralysis in his face, he had difficulty communicating.

For three years he drifted, begging and stealing in order to survive. He was also raping, murdering and mutilating men and women along his path. Vacher committed nearly all his murders by first cutting the throats of his victims. Afterwards he would slice open their torsos. Many of Vacher's victims were shepherds and shepherdesses; most were adolescents. His weapons were cleavers, scissors and knives – whatever happened to be at hand.

His actions soon drew the attention of authorities, who dubbed their elusive killer 'L'Éventreur du Sud-Est' – 'The Ripper of the South-East'.

In 1895, he was almost caught when he was spotted by a gendarme walking near a recently murdered shepherd boy. When called upon to produce identification, Vacher handed over his discharge papers. The gendarme remarked that he had once served in the very same regiment. When he asked whether Vacher had seen any suspicious characters, the murderer replied that he had seen a man running across the fields about a mile away. The gendarme then set off in pursuit.

The killing came to an end in early August 1897 when Vacher happened upon a woman outside Lyons who was gathering wood. He attacked, but was immediately set upon by his intended victim's husband and sons. Vacher was arrested.

Although the authorities were convinced that Vacher was *L'Éventreur du Sud-Est*, they had neither witnesses nor evidence. Their big break came from Vacher himself, who one day, without explanation, chose to confess all his crimes.

He was, he argued, not responsible for his actions, owing to the dog that had given him rabies as a child. Vacher was convinced that his blood had been poisoned. It was because of this condition, Vacher claimed, that he felt an urge to drink blood from the necks of his victims. Hatred had also played a role in his murders – hatred brought on by those who found his deformed face unsightly.

Vacher was tried with what appears to have been undue haste. He was examined by a team of doctors who determined that the memory of the accused was clear. The fact that he had fled the scene of each murder was, they claimed, an indication that he was fully cognizant of the difference between right and wrong. Among those who examined Vacher was Alexandre Lacassagne, a professor of forensic medicine at the Université de Lyon. He later wrote a book, *Vacher l'éventreur et les crimes sadiques*, in which he drew comparisons between the serial killer and figures like Gilles de Rais and Jack the Ripper.

On 28 October 1898, after a trial which lasted two days, Vacher was sentenced to death. Two months later, on New Year's Eve, he was guillotined at Bourg-en-Bresse, not far from where he had performed his military service.

DOCTOR H. H. HOLMES

It is not correct, as is often claimed, that H. H. Holmes was America's first serial killer; both the Bloody Benders (a Kansas family of serial killers) and the Servant Girl Annihilator preceded him. He did, however, kill more people than the Servant Girl Annihilator and all the members of the Bender family put together. The claim that Holmes was the most prolific American serial killer of all time remains an issue of some debate.

The man who history remembers as H. H. Holmes was born Herman Webster Mudgett on 16 May 1860 in Gilmanton, New Hampshire. Nearly a century and a half later, the town numbers barely more than 3,000 inhabitants. It is perhaps most famous as having served as a model for Grace Metalious's Peyton Place, the setting for the 1956 novel of the same name.

Holmes grew up in an impoverished family with an abusive alcoholic father at its head. School provided only a partial escape. While an intelligent and handsome boy, he was also a frequent victim of bullying. He once claimed that, as a child, he had been forced by his classmates to touch a human skeleton. It was an event that appeared to haunt him for the rest of his life. Nevertheless, he sought to become a medical doctor and developed a fascination with anatomy. As an adolescent, this interest found expression in his killing and dismembering of stray animals.

At 16, he graduated from school and managed to get teaching positions – first in Gilmanton and later in nearby Alton, New Hampshire. It was there that he met Clara Lovering. The ardour between them was such that the two eloped. However, in marriage that same passion quickly dissipated and he soon abandoned his wife.

Still intent on a career in medicine, he attended the University of Vermont. It was, however, too small for his liking. In September 1882, he enrolled at the University of Michigan at Ann Arbor, which held what was considered to be one of the country's leading medical schools. Two years later, he graduated with what are best described as lacklustre grades.

After graduation, Mudgett adopted as his name the more distinguished sounding Henry Howard Holmes. He took up a position as prescription clerk in a pharmacy owned by a terminally ill doctor named Holton. He endeared himself to Holton's wife and customers. When the good doctor passed away, Holmes offered to buy the pharmacy, promising the newly made widow $100 a month. After signing over the deed, Mrs Holton subsequently disappeared; Holmes claimed she had settled with relatives in California.

Under Holmes, the pharmacy thrived in the growing Englewood neighbourhood of Chicago. In 1887, he married Myrta Z. Belknap, a stunning young woman whom he had met during a business trip to Minneapolis. She remained unaware that Holmes had been married before – and that he had not

Herman Webster Mudgett, aka H. H. Holmes, was a notorious insurance murderer who killed up to 27 people, many of them at the World's Columbian Exposition of 1893. He was executed in 1895

obtained a divorce. In their third year of marriage, Myrta bore a daughter named Lucy. By this time she had already returned to the home of her parents. Though Holmes would never seek a divorce, the union was all but over.

Using the pharmacy as his base, Holmes continued to engage in a number of questionable business ventures he had begun several years before. However, his most notable achievement was the construction of a block-long, three-storey building on the site across the street from his pharmacy. Built over a three-year period, 'The Castle', as the locals dubbed it, included a ground floor which Holmes rented out to various shopkeepers. The upper two storeys Holmes kept for himself. A huge space, it was a confusing maze of over a hundred windowless rooms, secret passageways, false floors and stairways that led to nowhere. Some doors could only be opened from the outside, while others opened to reveal nothing but a brick wall. During construction, Holmes repeatedly changed contractors, ensuring that no one understood the design of the building or had any idea as to its ultimate purpose.

Beginning shortly after the completion of the Castle, and for the three years that followed, Holmes murdered dozens of women. Some he tortured in soundproof chambers fitted with gas lines that enabled him to asphyxiate his victims. The corpses were sent down a secret chute to the Castle's basement. There, Holmes would dissect them, just as he had the animals he killed in his adolescence. They would be stripped of flesh and sold as skeleton models to medical schools. Some bodies were cremated or thrown in pits of lime and acid.

The venue for the World's Columbian Exposition held in Chicago to celebrate the 400th anniversary of Christopher Columbus's discovery of America – Holmes opened up his own World's Fair Hotel and started to pick off his guests

One of the first to die was Julia Connor, the wife of a jeweller to whom Holmes had rented a shop. After she came to Holmes with the news that she was pregnant with his child, the doctor murdered Julia and her daughter, Pearl.

Holmes saw great opportunity in Chicago's upcoming 1893 World's Columbian Exposition and made several modifications to the second storey of the Castle, transforming it into the World's Fair Hotel. The first guests arrived in the spring of 1893. Some returned home, others did not. With the high volume of guests, Holmes could be selective in choosing his victims. The fact that so many people were coming to the fair without any place to stay ensured that his activities went unnoticed.

One of those who remained alive was Georgiana Yorke, who became Holmes' third wife in January 1894. She believed Holmes to be a very wealthy man, with property in Texas and Europe. Indeed, he appeared to be quite prosperous. However, his debts had begun to catch up with him.

After having been confronted by his creditors, he came up with a scheme which involved a man named Benjamin Pietzel. As a carpenter, Pietzel had worked on the Castle. Exactly how much he knew of Holmes' activities is a matter of some debate. What is certain is that Pietzel agreed to fake his own death in order to collect a large insurance claim. In the end, Holmes simply killed the man and kept all the money for himself. He then made off with three of Pietzel's children.

On 17 November 1894, having been on the road for nearly two years, Holmes was arrested in Boston. Initially, he was suspected of nothing more than fraud. However, an insurance agent's diligence in attempting to track down the three Pietzel children revealed that they had been killed in the cities of Indianapolis and Toronto. This news encouraged the police in Chicago to investigate Holmes' Castle. On 20 July 1895, all was revealed. The police spent a month investigating what some now called 'the Murder Castle' before, on 19 August, it was consumed by a fire of mysterious origin.

Exactly how many poor souls Holmes murdered is a mystery. The number has typically been estimated as being between 20 and 100. The authorities put the murder count at 27, committed in Chicago, Philadelphia, Indianapolis and Toronto. The police in Chicago noted that many of the bodies in the basement of the Castle had been dissected and burnt to such an extent that it was difficult to determine precisely how many bodies it contained. At his trial, Holmes confessed to 27 murders.

Holmes was led to the gallows on the morning of 7 May 1896. As he watched the preparations for his hanging, he is reported to have said, 'Take your time; don't bungle it.' However, despite the hangman's care, Holmes died an agonizing death. For ten minutes after the trapdoor was sprung, his body twitched. He was officially pronounced dead after he had been hanging for 15 minutes.

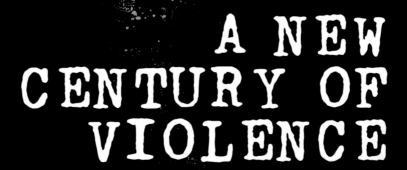

A NEW CENTURY OF VIOLENCE

The early part of the 20th century saw war fought on a previously unimaginable scale in the air and in trenches. Chemical warfare was employed, civilians became targets, and stories of horrific atrocities were spread as propaganda. By the end of the fighting, more than nine million civilians and soldiers had been killed. Perhaps it was contagious. As if a reflection of the war, incidents of psychopathic killing rapidly increased.

BÉLA KISS

Béla Kiss was one of the most loved and respected men in the small Hungarian town of Cinkota. When he left to fight for the Austro-Hungarian army in the First World War, many townsfolk prayed for his safe return.

Kiss had lived in Cinkota, a part of present-day Budapest, since 1900. A handsome blue-eyed, blond-haired 23-year-old, married to a beautiful woman named Marie, his arrival in the town had not gone unnoticed. Kiss and his wife rented a house on the outskirts of town, from which he practised as a tinsmith. He'd taught himself the trade and, in fact, had had no formal schooling whatsoever. The impressive and expansive knowledge he possessed in the areas of art, literature, history and astronomy was the result of years of independent study. Among the inhabitants of Cinkota, he was considered a highly educated young man. Kiss was also known for his generosity; though dedicated and hard-working, he was famous locally for the wonderful parties he would hold at the local hotel.

Town gossips, however, became aware that things weren't quite as they appeared. Marie had begun having an affair with an artist. In 1912, Kiss announced that she had run off with her lover. Overnight, Kiss was transformed from jilted husband to the most desirable bachelor in town.

Kiss hired one Mrs Jakubec, a housekeeper, to care for his home while he focused on his trade. He also entered into correspondences with several young women. It was not long before a number of single, attractive women began visiting his Cinkota home. This steady parade prompted gossip of a different sort. As each woman passed through town on the way to the tinsmith's home,

Béla Kiss was the talk of the town in Cinkota, Hungary and considered quite a catch. Women queued up to meet him when he announced in 1912 that his wife had left him after an affair with an artist

In 1914 Kiss left Cinkota to serve in the Austro-Hungarian army and was never heard of again, though rumours continued to circulate and further sightings were reported, one as late as 1932 when he was 'seen' in New York

there was speculation as to whether this might be the next Mrs Kiss. It seemed, however, that Kiss was having no luck in finding a suitable mate – most women were seen in his company only once. Mrs Jakubec would later say that she had never had the opportunity to know any of her employer's visitors.

By the latter half of 1914, when Kiss left to serve in the First World War, no replacement for the unfaithful Marie had been found.

Mrs Jakubec was left alone in the house, and yet neither she nor the townsfolk heard anything from Kiss. As the war progressed, rumours began to circulate that the popular figure had been taken as a prisoner of war. There was some speculation that Kiss had been killed in some unnamed battle. By the end of the second year, the lease had lapsed on the house Kiss had begun renting some 16 years before.

It was at this point that a rather gruesome discovery was made – one that transformed Kiss from a thoroughly respected citizen of Cinkota into the town's greatest monster.

Although there are two very different accounts of the events leading up to Kiss's unmasking, both involve six sealed metal drums that he had lined up outside his home. One story relies on the memory of something Kiss had supposedly told a town constable. When asked, in the early months of 1914, what the mysterious metal drums contained, the tinsmith revealed that he was hoarding petrol in the anticipation that war would soon be declared. In this version, the constable, thinking the fuel would be of use in the fighting, contacted the military, who, in turn, prised open the drums.

The other story has it that Kiss's landlord came upon the drums while preparing to rent out the property. Curious as to their contents, he punctured one of the drums and was met with a nauseating smell. Kiss's neighbour, a chemist, was convinced that the scent was that of rotting human flesh. According to this version, it was the authorities who, under Charles Nagy, the chief detective of the Budapest police, opened the drums.

Whatever the chain of events, both led to the same horrible discovery: each drum contained the corpse of a naked young woman. A search of the property Kiss had rented revealed a further 18 bodies, including that of the adulterous Marie Kiss. All 24 victims had been preserved in wood alcohol, which aided greatly in identification

Nagy immediately informed the military, advising that Kiss be arrested. Mrs Jakubec, who had protested so strongly against the drums being opened, was detained. Suspicion of the housekeeper deepened when it was discovered that she was the main beneficiary in Kiss's will. Proclaiming her innocence, Mrs Jakubec led police to a room her employer had forbidden her to enter. It was no chamber of horrors – no further bodies were found, as some had expected. Indeed, Kiss's forbidden room, containing a few bookcases, a large desk and a chair, at first looked quite innocent. However, its sinister purpose was quickly revealed.

The bookcases were filled with volumes on the subjects of strangulation and poisons. The desk held correspondence with 74 women, including letters going back as far as 13 years. There were marriage proposals, love letters and photographs. Through notices he'd placed in the personal columns of various newspapers, Kiss had been swindling women who were seeking husbands.

The tinsmith had selected his victims with great care. Each victim met two criteria: an abundance of wealth and an absence of relatives. In other words, he desired moneyed women who would not be missed if they happened to disappear.

Among his victims was Katerine Varga, a very wealthy young widow who sold a thriving dressmaking business in order to be with her prospective husband in Cinkota.

The mother of another young woman, Margaret Toth, had given Kiss money after he had promised to marry her daughter. On a subsequent visit to Cinkota, the fiancé forced the young Miss Toth to write to her mother with the news that she was running off to the United States. Evidence indicates that Kiss then strangled the young woman and posted the letter.

Not all of Kiss's victims had been killed. It seemed that the metal drums and burial on the Cinkota property represented a fate that befell only women who had become troublesome. Indeed, records indicated that two of Kiss's victims, Julianne Paschek and Elizabeth Komeromi, had initiated separate court actions after he had taken their money under false pretences. The bodies of both complainants were found buried close to his home.

On 4 October 1916, as Nagy's investigation was set to enter the third month, the detective received word from a Serbian hospital that in 1915 Kiss had succumbed to typhoid. Shortly after, a second message arrived from Serbia, stating that Kiss was alive, recuperating in the very same institution. Nagy travelled immediately to the hospital, arriving to find a corpse in Kiss's bed – the body of a dead soldier who was quite obviously not the murderer. Nagy was certain that Kiss had somehow been tipped off and had hoped to throw off the police by placing a dead man in his bed.

While the tinsmith may not have been successful in fooling the chief detective of Budapest, his escape was effective. The trail was cold, and was warmed only occasionally by rumour and speculation. In 1919, he was supposedly spotted in Budapest. The following year, it was reported that he was serving under the alias 'Hoffman' in the French Foreign Legion.

One unconfirmed report was that he was in a Romanian prison, serving time on a charge of burglary; another had it that Kiss had died in Turkey of yellow fever.

The most intriguing of all these sightings occurred in 1932 when a New York Police Department homicide detective named Henry Oswald thought he saw Kiss exiting the Times Square subway station. Known as 'Camera Eye', owing to his flawless memory for faces, Oswald followed the man he thought was Kiss, but lost him in the crowd. He never saw the man again.

Kiss marched off with the army, but did he move on to the Foreign Legion?

THE AXEMAN OF NEW ORLEANS

On the evening of 19 March 1919, residents of New Orleans sat in bars and restaurants, listening to live bands, confident that the music being played, jazz, was protecting them from violent murder. It was just one of many evenings made bizarre by the Axeman of New Orleans, a serial killer who, literally and figuratively, struck randomly in Louisiana's largest city in the early part of the 20th century.

The mystery of the Axeman of New Orleans begins in two modest flats that once stood at the back of a grocery store at the corner of Upperline and Magnolia streets. In one flat lived Andrew Maggio, a barber, and his brother Jake. The other served as home to a third brother, Joseph, and Catherine, his wife. It was, in fact, Joseph and Catherine's grocery store and bar that separated the flats from the street. In the early hours of 23 May 1918, Jake was awoken by a sound, a sort of groaning, coming from Joseph and Catherine's apartment. At first, he tried to get the couple's attention by knocking on the wall. There was no response. He woke Andrew and together the two brothers went over to the adjacent flat.

They immediately came upon the sign of a break-in: a wooden panel that had been chiselled out of the kitchen door. Entering the apartment by the same point as the intruder, the pair rushed to the bedroom. There, they came upon Catherine. Lying across the bed, her skull was caved in, and her throat was so deeply cut that she was very nearly decapitated. Beneath their sister-in-law, bathed in her blood, lay their brother Joseph. He, too, had been attacked. His head was cut open in several places, yet the grocer was still alive. When he saw

New Orleans, Louisiana's largest city, was the hunting ground of 'the Axeman' in the early part of the last century

his brothers, Joseph attempted to stand, but found he could not. He died before an ambulance could be summoned.

After the authorities arrived, a pile of men's clothing was discovered on the bathroom floor. A bloody straight razor and an axe were also discovered. The coroner had no doubt that both had been used in killing the couple. The motive for the crime was less clear. Although the Maggios' safe was found to be open and empty, money placed in other locations in the flat, including a sum discovered beneath Joseph's pillow, was left behind.

The horrific scene ensured that the murders of Joseph and Catherine Maggio were front-page news. Public interest was further aroused when it was learned that the razor used in the crime belonged to Andrew Maggio. He claimed he had taken it home from his barber shop on the very evening of the murders in order to repair a small nick in the blade. He was arrested, but released for lack of evidence. The axe, it was determined, had belonged to the murdered couple.

It was during Andrew's brief time in custody that the case took the first of what would be a number of peculiar turns. Two detectives came across a message scrawled in chalk on the pavement less than a block from where the couple had been murdered. It read: 'Mrs Maggio will sit up tonight just like Mrs Toney.'

Rumours began to circulate that the Maggio murder had been committed by the same hand that had killed a number of New Orleans grocers six years earlier. Some said it was the work of the Mafia and that 'Mrs Toney' was a reference to the wife of Tony Schiambra. In 1911, both he and his wife had been killed by a murderer who had used an axe.

Two weeks after the Maggio murders, baker John Zanca stumbled over a scene not at all dissimilar to that discovered by the bereaved brothers. Early on the morning of 6 June, Zanca arrived with his regular delivery of fresh bread at

A typical New Orleans grocery around the time of the killings. His mistress claimed grocer Louis Besumer had attacked her although they had both been assaulted with an axe. After a brief trial he was found not guilty

Louis Besumer's grocery store and was surprised to find the storefront dark. Looking through the window, he saw no sign of life, and so walked around the building and knocked on the side door. It was opened almost immediately by Besumer. His face was covered in blood. Besumer's mistress, Anna Lowe, was lying in their bed, unable to move. They had both been attacked with an axe. Despite primitive medical treatment, the grocer managed to survive. His mistress was not so lucky. After clinging to life for a further two months, she died

on 5 August, but not before claiming that it was Besumer who had attacked her. The grocer was arrested and, after a brief trial, found not guilty.

That very same day, shortly after midnight, the next attack occurred. The victim was a Mrs Edward Schneider, who awoke to find a dark figure standing over her bed. The intruder attacked her with an axe, hitting her several times in the face. Discovered by her husband, Mrs Schneider not only survived, but three weeks later gave birth to a healthy baby girl.

A pattern, it seemed, had been established. A killer, wielding an axe, was attacking people as they slept. He usually gained access to his victims by chiselling out door panels.

On 10 August, an elderly man by the name of Joseph Romano was killed. His niece, Pauline Bruno, reported seeing a dark figure in the house. He turned and fled her room after she had let out a scream.

For a time, it almost seemed as if Pauline Bruno's scream had scared off the killer completely. Then, seven months later, in the early hours of 10 March 1919, the Axeman of New Orleans struck again. As in the past, the victims, grocers Charles and Rosie Cortimiglia, and their 2-year-old daughter Mary, were attacked as they slept. Mary, asleep in her mother's arms, died instantly from a single blow to the back of the head. Charles struggled with the attacker, but was felled by several blows to the torso. Rosie, too, received wounds, primarily to the head.

Three days later, the editor of the *Times-Picayune* received a letter from someone who signed himself 'The Axeman'. Describing himself as 'a spirit and a fell demon from the hottest hell', the correspondent announced that he would strike again 'at 12:15 (earthly time) on next Tuesday night', before offering a magnanimous gesture:

'I am very fond of jazz music, and I swear by all the devils in the nether regions that every person shall be spared in whose home a jazz band is in full swing at the time I have mentioned. If everyone has a jazz band going, well, then, so much the better for you people. One thing is certain and that is that some of those people who do not jazz it on Tuesday night (if there be any) will get the axe.'

New Orleans is the home of jazz and the letter received at the Times-Picayune *threatened anybody who didn't want to dance*

That Tuesday the bars and restaurants of New Orleans were filled with patrons seeking safety from the self-described 'fell demon'. Even venues not at all known for playing jazz hired musicians for the night. There were no victims that evening.

After her recovery, Rosie Cortimiglia accused father and son Frank and Iolando Jordano, business rivals of her husband, of her daughter's murder. Some newspaper accounts record that Charles disputed his wife's accusation; others state that he died of his injuries. Whatever the case, he did not join his wife in testifying at the subsequent trial of the Jordanos. Frank was sentenced to death, while Iolando received a life sentence.

And yet the incarceration of the Jordanos, like those of Andrew Maggio and Louis Besumer, did nothing to stop the attacks. The Axeman's next victim was another grocer, Steve Boca, who was attacked as he slept on 10 August 1919. Boca survived his wounds. Once again, the assailant used a chisel to gain access to his lodgings.

He struck again three weeks later, on 3 September, using his axe on a sleeping 19-year-old woman named Sarah Laumann. She later died in the hospital.

Miss Laumann had been alone when attacked, but eight people were home when the next victim, Mike Pepitone, was attacked. One of the eight, Mrs Pepitone, reported seeing two intruders in her house. Her husband could provide no statement. He died shortly after arriving at Charity Hospital.

And it was here that the attacks ended.

The mystery of the Axeman of New Orleans may never be truly solved, but there were further events that may provide some indication of the truth. The first took place on 2 December 1919 when Mike Pepitone's widow stepped out of a darkened doorway and shot a man named Joseph Mumfre. She then waited next to his dead body. When the authorities arrived, Mrs Pepitone claimed that Mumfre was one of the two men she had seen fleeing her bedroom on the night of her husband's murder.

Five days later, on 7 December, Rosie Cortimiglia retracted her accusation against Frank and Iolando Jordano. They were summarily released from prison.

Whether Joseph Mumfre was the Axeman of New Orleans is a matter of considerable debate. A man with an unenviable criminal record, he had been in prison during the period between the last axe murder of 1911 and the first of 1918, and again between the murder of Joseph Romano on 10 August 1918 and that of Mary Cortimiglia seven months later.

Mrs Pepitone herself served three years for Mumfre's murder. She was never able to identify the second man she claimed to have seen on the evening of her husband's murder. It may well be that 'The Axeman' was right when he wrote in that infamous letter to the *Times-Picayune*: 'They have never caught me and they never will.'

HENRI LANDRU

Henri Landru was short and bald, with an unkempt beard and bushy eyebrows. Yet approximately 300 women in First World War France saw him as a desirable partner and an object of romance.

A Parisian from birth, Henri Désiré Landru entered the world on 12 April 1869. His mother took care of the home, while his father worked keeping the blast furnaces alive at the Forges de Vulcain, an ironworks located within the city. An intelligent if unexceptional boy, Landru attended Catholic school and, in later years, studied engineering. At the age of 18, he was drafted into the military. Here, too, he did well. By the time he was discharged four years later, he had achieved the rank of sergeant.

To all appearances, Landru had grown into a respectable, dependable young man, who attracted little attention. What little profile he had came from his service as a deacon in his church. He was also a member of the choir. It therefore seemed uncharacteristic when, in 1891, he seduced one of his cousins, Marie-Catherine Remi, impregnating her. Later that same year, she gave birth to a daughter. Two years passed before Landru did the honourable thing and married the mother of his child.

Shortly after the marriage, Landru entered the business world as a clerk. As his family began to expand, he was dealt a significant blow when his employer ran off to the United States, taking with him money Landru had provided as a bond. The swindle appears to have motivated Landru to act in kind.

He established a business dealing in used furniture and was soon preying on recently widowed women. Often Landru's victims would enter his shop, hoping to sell furniture in order to supplement the modest pensions left them by their departed husbands. Landru would then encourage these women to invest these same pensions, stealing their money in the process. The cons went unnoticed for some time until, in 1900, he was arrested after having attempted to withdraw funds using a false identity. It was the first in a series of seven convictions.

Landru spent the first decade of the 20th century moving in and out of prison. The longest sentence received was for a scheme that began with a matrimonial advertisement he'd placed in a Lille newspaper. Portraying himself as a wealthy widower, he had persuaded one respondent, a 40-year-old widow named Jeanne Isoré, to exchange 15,000 francs for several counterfeit deeds. By the time the law caught up with Landru, the money was long gone – Mme Isoré was impoverished.

Landru's lawlessness had also taken a toll on his family. His mother died while he was in prison. Landru's father, ashamed of his son's behaviour, committed suicide. Landru's wife and four children were penniless.

By the beginning of 1914, he had become estranged from his wife, although

Henri Landru preyed on recently widowed women who came into his second-hand furniture shop hoping to sell their furnishings in order to supplement the modest pensions they had been left by their departed husbands no divorce was sought. During the tensions leading up to the First World War, Landru was released, yet again, from prison. After spending his initial months of freedom drifting around the French countryside, he somehow ended up in a rented villa on the outskirts of Paris. During one trip into the city he met a very attractive 39-year-old named Jeanne Cuchet. A widow, she was employed in a lingerie shop and had a 16-year-old son named André.

Though a romance developed quickly between Cuchet and the man she knew as Raymond Diard, the couple hit at least one rough patch. When this occurred, the distraught woman's family accompanied her to meet with the suitor at his villa. Finding he wasn't at home, Cuchet's brother-in-law took the opportunity to investigate the suave Diard. He searched the villa and came across a chest containing letters from other women. The family was outraged, but not so Cuchet herself. She severed ties with her relatives, and with André moved into Diard's villa.

In January 1915, the three relocated to a villa in Vernouillet, after which the mother and son were never seen again. It is thought that their bodies were incinerated in their new home. Shortly after the Cuchets disappeared, Landru opened a bank account with 5,000 francs, an amount he claimed he had inherited from his late father. He also presented his estranged wife with a gold watch that had once belonged to Jeanne Cuchet.

Another lady, Thérèse Laborde-Line, vanished in July 1915. A wealthy Argentine widow, she and Landru had set up house in a lovely new villa shortly before her disappearance. He later returned to collect her furniture.

In May, two months earlier, as M. Fréymet, Landru had placed a newspaper advertisement in Paris' *Le Journal*: 'Widower with two children, aged 43, with comfortable income, serious and moving in good society, desires to meet widow with a view to matrimony.'

Nearly everything about the advertisement was a lie: Landru was not a widower, he had four children, he had no income and he had no contact with anything that could be described as 'good society'. Even his age was a lie – Landru was in his forty-sixth year. However, while it wasn't true that he desired matrimony, he was most certainly interested in meeting a widow.

And he met many.

In August 1915, a 51-year-old widow named Marie Angelique Desirée Pelletier disappeared. She was soon followed by a Mme Héon, Mme Buisson, Mme Collomb, Mme Jaume and Mme Pascal.

Two victims stand out from the rest. The first, Andrée Babelay, was a 19-year-old servant girl who had no money. Why Landru killed her remains a mystery. It may be that she somehow discovered his secret.

The second, Marie-Thérèse Marchadier, was not a widow. That said, she did have money. In fact, she had become something of a celebrity during the war as an entertainer for the troops known as 'La Belle Mythese'.

Marchadier vanished without trace at about the time of the Armistice.

With 'La Belle Mythese', Landru had claimed his 11th murder victim, and still no one suspected him of any wrongdoing.

The end of Landru's killing came about through an unrelated death. Late in 1918, the son of Mme Buisson died. The family attempted to reach the mother, care of a M. Fremiet in Gambais, with whom, it was thought, she had run off. They heard back from the mayor that the town had no M. Fremiet. He suggested that the family might wish to contact the family of Mme Collomb, another woman who was believed to have gone missing in Gambais.

Clearly Landru sensed that, after all these years, a net was slowly closing. He left Gambais for good, moving in with his 27-year-old mistress in Paris. The authorities arrived to find his villa unoccupied.

However, the family of Mme Buisson was not so easily defeated. For months, Buisson's sister haunted the streets of the Parisian neighbourhood in which she had once been introduced to the mysterious M. Fremiet. On 12 April 1919, her dedication paid off when she spotted her sister's suitor entering a porcelain shop. Finally, the authorities managed to catch up with Landru. When arrested, he was found to be carrying a notebook containing names and details of 283 women, including nearly all of the widows who had gone missing.

Despite the discovery of the notebook, police were unable to charge Landru with anything more than embezzlement. Simply put, there were no bodies. The properties surrounding his villas in Gambais and Vernouillet were dug up, but revealed nothing more than the bones of two dogs. Landru admitted to strangling both at the request of the owner, Marie-Thérèse Marchadier.

A furnace Landru had installed shortly after moving into the Gambais villa provided the damning evidence. It had sat there completely ignored for much of the investigation, until neighbours remembered the black smoke and noxious fumes that had on occasion spewed out of the villa's chimney. The bones and teeth found behind the iron door of the furnace finally provided the evidence needed to proceed in charging Landru with 11 counts of murder.

On 25 February 1922 Henri Landau kneeled beneath the blade of the guillotine and departed this life

Charlie Chaplin and Marilyn Nash in Monsieur Verdoux, *a film about a banker who loses his job and starts marrying – and murdering – wealthy widows. This was inspired by Henri Landru and his exploits*

His trial began on 7 November 1921. Arrogant and impudent, Landru's demeanour in no way supported his defence. He admitted nothing and argued that the prosecution had proved his innocence in claiming him to be a sane man. Despite this, the victims' families and members of the jury presented the court with a petition requesting mercy. This was ignored and on 30 November 1921, Landru was sentenced to death.

On 25 February 1922, he kneeled beneath the blade of a guillotine and was executed.

In 1947, 25 years after the end of Henri Landru, his life was resurrected as the inspiration for the main character of Charlie Chaplin's *Monsieur Verdoux*. Played by the actor, Verdoux is a banker who, after having been dismissed, supports his family by marrying and murdering wealthy widows.

In 1963, the murderer returned to the screen in a more direct form, a feature film centred on his crimes entitled *Landru*. Directed by Claude Chabrol, the movie occasioned a lawsuit from an elderly woman named Fernande Segret – the Parisian mistress to whom Landru had fled in 1918. Upset by her portrayal in the film, she sought 200,000 francs in damages. She was awarded 10,000 francs in 1965. Three years later, the 74-year-old woman committed suicide in a very dramatic fashion by jumping into the moat of the Château de Flers in Orne. She left behind a note reading: 'I still love him, but I am suffering too greatly. I am going to kill myself.'

FRITZ HAARMANN

Fritz Haarmann recognized the social unrest, hyperinflation and food shortages experienced by Germany in the years after the First World War and used them to his advantage. He preyed on runaways and male prostitutes. Convicted of having murdered 24 boys and young men, it is more likely that he killed over 50. Together with his live-in lover, he sold the clothing and meagre belongings

of his victims in a public market. But that was not the only profit Haarmann made from his killings; he also sold their flesh as steak on the black market. During his time, Haarmann was known by many names, including the Vampire of Hanover and the Werewolf of Hanover; but history has settled on the most appropriate: The Butcher of Hanover.

Friedrich Heinrich Karl Haarmann was born on 25 October 1879 in Hanover. It might be said that during his early life he was something of a stereotype. The youngest of six children, he was coddled by his mother and disliked by his father. The young Fritz loved to play with dolls, and avoided more masculine pastimes. Although he shunned team sports, he was athletic and excelled in gymnastics. He was attracted to the feminine, while demonstrating abhorrence for the masculine.

As a young man, one of his brothers was arrested and sentenced for a sexual assault. As a teenager, Haarmann himself got in trouble with the law after molesting a number of children. At the age of 18, after a thorough examination, he was sent to an asylum. It wasn't long before he managed to escape.

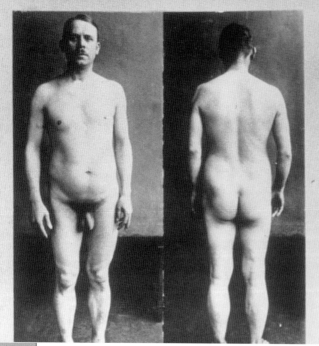

Police pictures of Fritz Haarmann: he was coddled by his mother and disliked by his father

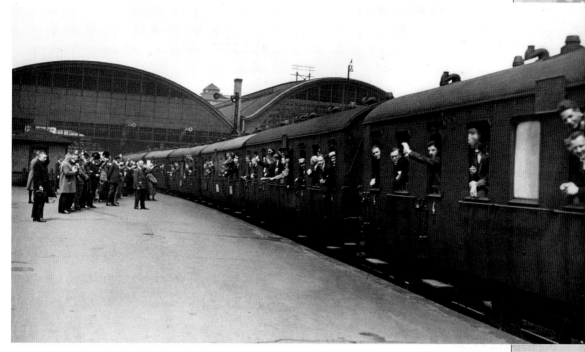

Hanover station in 1926, some years after it had become a favourite haunt of Fritz Haarmann. Here it was that he could pick up society's waifs and strays, displaced by the First World War and its long, desperate aftermath

Haarmann fled to Switzerland, but by the age of 21 had returned to Hanover. Within months he had married and impregnated a woman named Erna Loewart. However, before the birth, Haarmann had again moved on, deserting his wife to join the army. His role as a soldier proved to be as brief as had been the role of husband. Deemed unsuitable for service, Haarmann was soon back living with the father he so detested. What followed was a period consisting of smuggling, thievery and a variety of sexual offences. Over the next decade, one in three years was spent in prison.

Exactly when he began killing is unknown. The first known incident connecting Haarmann with murder occurred in September 1918, when police burst into his apartment. They were looking for a young runaway named Friedel Roth. What they found instead was Haarmann in bed with a young boy. Although he was arrested and sentenced to nine months in prison, Haarmann likely thought that being caught molesting the boy had been a lucky break. In dealing with the paedophiliac crime, the authorities neglected the initial purpose of their visit: the investigation of Friedel Roth's disappearance. Had they bothered to search Haarmann's room, the police would have discovered the runaway boy's severed head wrapped in newspaper behind the stove.

The threat of imprisonment appears to have had no effect on Haarmann. As he awaited sentencing, he returned to the streets, parks and squares of Hanover, looking to have sex with boys and young men. His favourite hunting spot, however, was the city's main railway station. It had always been a fertile territory, made even more so by the economic upheavals of the First World War and its aftermath. During one visit, sometime around his 40th birthday in the autumn of 1919, Haarmann was approached by a young male prostitute named Hans Grans. It would not be fair to say that Grans was everything Haarmann was not, but there certainly was a contrast. The middle-aged Haarmann was a pleasant-enough-looking man. Average in height, with a round face described as friendly-looking, he wouldn't have stood out in a crowd. Grans, on the other hand, was remarkably handsome, with the chiselled blond features that would later come to be idealized and exploited by the Nazis. Although Grans was less than half Haarmann's age, the two soon became constant lovers and close friends.

In March 1920, Haarmann finally began the nine-month sentence stemming from the police raid that had taken place 19 months earlier. Grans spent the remainder of the year roaming about Germany, supporting himself through thievery and prostitution. The two were reunited on Christmas Day and soon thereafter moved into an apartment together. They appeared as two respectable, well-dressed men, all the while stealing laundry from clothes lines. Their ill-gotten gains were sold in the market across from the station in which they had

> **Fritz Franke was made to accompany Haarmann. When Grans arrived home later, the body of the dead boy was lying in the room**

first met. Haarmann further contributed to the household finances through a disability pension. While the state may have considered him unable to work, Haarmann found employment with the local police. This man, whom the authorities had sent to prison the previous year, became one of their most valuable informers – Haarmann appeared to have no hesitation when it came to turning people in. As hyperinflation and economic collapse caused turmoil in the lives of their neighbours, Haarmann and Grans managed to maintain a comfortable, if modest, lifestyle in their little one-room Neuestrasse apartment.

Whether Grans knew of his partner's 1918 murder of Friedel Roth is a matter of speculation. What is certain is that by early 1923, the prostitute knew his partner to be a murderer. In February, Haarmann detained two boys in his favourite train station. The less attractive of the pair he dismissed. The other, Fritz Franke, was made to accompany Haarmann to his home. When Grans arrived home later in the day, the body of the dead boy was lying in the room.

From this point, the murders continued at a frequent and steady pace.

Haarmann's method had little variation and was extremely effective. On some occasions he would pick up boys by offering employment or a place to stay. Other incidents would begin with Haarmann approaching his victims with the claim that he was a police officer. The latter pretence was used so frequently, and with such effect, that at least one guard at the station thought Haarmann was a police detective.

SEXUAL FRENZY

The boys would then be taken to the Neuestrasse apartment where Haarmann would kill them by biting through their throats in a moment of sexual frenzy.

As he preyed on runaways, it was quite some time before the authorities began to suspect that something untoward was taking place. It wasn't until 17 May 1924, when a skull was found by children playing along the Leine, that the fate of missing children and young men began to become apparent. Within a month, three more skulls had been discovered along the riverbank. Autopsies indicated that they belonged to young males ranging in age from 12 to 20 years. Following the discovery of a sack filled with human bones, the Leine was dammed and the riverbed inspected by police and municipal workers. Over 500 body parts were found.

Haarmann, like the whole city of Hanover, was well aware of the investigation. Although he was on the police payroll as an informer, he was among the suspects. In fact, he was investigated in May and again in June – but still he continued to kill. His last known murder took place in June 1924. The victim was a young man named Erich de Vries, whom he had picked up at the train station with an offer of cigarettes.

As many of the disappeared had last been seen at the train station, the site became a focus of the investigation. In June, two of the youngest members of the force were sent by train from Berlin to Hanover. By pretending to be homeless, it was hoped that they would come into contact with the killer.

The luck that had six years earlier prevented the discovery of Friedel Roth's severed head returned to Haarmann. At the station, the murderer met with a 15-year-old boy named Karl Fromm, who had once stayed with Haarmann and Grans. Irritated by the boy's attitude, Haarmann sought to make things difficult by claiming to railway police that the boy was travelling under false papers. Fromm turned the tables on his former host by charging that he had been molested during his stay at the Neuestrasse apartment. As the young police officers waited in the train station, hoping to be approached by the killer, Haarmann was arrested.

As he was still a suspect in the disappearances, police took the opportunity to search Haarmann and Grans' apartment. There they found clothing belonging to many of the missing and murdered boys. While Haarmann admitted to having sex with several of the missing boys, he maintained that he'd had nothing to do with their disappearances. He insisted that the items of clothing, which numbered in the hundreds, were just a part of his business as a dealer in used clothes. Gradually, however, evidence from other quarters was being gathered. Among those connecting the clothing dealer to the murders was a boy named Fritz Kahlmeyer who identified Haarmann as the police officer who had accompanied him and his friend to a local circus on the evening of the latter's disappearance.

After weeks of interrogation, with evidence mounting, Haarmann confessed.

On 8 July 1924, 15 days after Haarmann's arrest, police took Grans into custody.

The subsequent trial, beginning on 8 December 1924, was as spectacular as it was bizarre. Haarmann conducted his own defence in a casual manner, as if oblivious to the seriousness of the charges. Smiling, he told little jokes, smoked a cigar and complained about the number of women in the courtroom. As always, Grans appeared in stark contrast. Charged with two counts of murder, he was serious and intense. The two men turned on each other, the bitterness escalating after Haarmann accused his former lover of taking part in certain murders. When the trial drew to an end nine days later, both men received death sentences.

Haarmann and Grans shared a room in the Neuestrasse apartment and Haarmann would invite runaways there. He used to pretend he was a police officer to lure them to his lair and then do away with them

What followed was a twist worthy of de Maupassant. While working one day, a messenger came across a letter lying on a Hanover street. Addressed and ultimately delivered to Albert Grans, the father of Hans, the letter was a lengthy and detailed confession from Fritz Haarmann in which he, the Butcher of Hanover, revealed that he had framed his former lover. After his father passed the letter on to the authorities, Grans was retried and received a sentence of 12 years.

On 15 April 1925, Haarmann was beheaded. His life and crimes were adapted to the screen in the 1973 Ulli Lommel film *Die Zärtlichkeit der Wölfe* (The Tenderness of the Wolves). In 1995, Haarmann's story returned to the screen in *Der Totmacher* (The Deathmaker). Starring Götz George, the script often uses the Butcher's own words as recorded in the files of Erich Schultze, one of the psychiatric experts who interviewed Haarmann during his last days.

But what of Hans Grans? After his release from prison he returned to Hanover, where it seems he probably lived out the rest of his life. He is known to have been living in the city as late as the 1970s.

EARLE NELSON

In Edgar Allan Poe's classic 1841 short story 'The Murders in the Rue Morgue', detective C. Auguste Dupin is baffled by the strangulation of two women in what appears to be an inaccessible room off a street in Paris. His conclusion? The deaths were suffered at the hands of an orang-utan, the escaped pet of a French sailor. Earle Nelson's victims were also women – at least 20, murdered in both the United States and Canada. Like Poe's orang-utan, Nelson killed with his hands. Such was his strength that he earned the moniker 'The Gorilla Man'.

It cannot be said that Earle Leonard Nelson ever really knew his mother and father; both died of syphilis within 18 months of his birth on 12 May 1897. He was raised by his widowed grandmother in San Francisco, the city in which he was born. A devout Pentecostal, Jennie Nelson was described as a distant woman. Most of her time and energy was spent in a constant struggle to maintain a household which included Earle and two of her own children. Nelson picked up on his grandmother's religious devotion, developing something of an obsession with the Bible. This did nothing to prevent him stealing from shopkeepers or behaving badly at school. He was expelled for the first time at the age of 7.

Four years later, Nelson suffered a horrific accident which some speculate may have contributed to his actions later in life. Riding a bicycle, he passed in front of a streetcar and was hit. He landed on his head, creating a wound that left him unconscious. It wasn't until ten days later that he was able to leave his bed.

Always a poor student, at 14 years of age Nelson left school for good. During the same year, his grandmother died and he went to live with his Aunt Lillian and her husband. He began to work, but seemed incapable of maintaining employment. Often he would simply wander away from a job, never to return. Although his aunt would later say that he was like a child in this respect, Nelson soon adopted some very adult habits. When he was 15 years old, he began to drink heavily and frequent the brothels of the city's Barbary Coast district. He would go out on binges for days – even weeks – at a time. These disappearances, Nelson explained to his aunt and uncle, were simply a result of his looking for work. Indeed, he always managed to contribute financially to the household. However, in the spring of 1915, a partial explanation for their nephew's absences was revealed when Nelson was caught after burgling a cabin in northern California. At 18, he was sentenced to two years at San Quentin Prison.

An illustration by Aubrey Beardsley for 'The Murders in the Rue Morgue'

His release took place in April 1917, just weeks after the United States entered the First World War. Nelson enlisted under his name at birth, Earle Leonard Ferral, but soon lost interest. Mere weeks after enlisting, he went AWOL. Nelson made his way to Salt Lake City where, rather incredibly, he enlisted in the United States Navy. By May, he was in San Francisco, working as a cook at the Mare Island Naval Base. He again deserted. However, these two experiences did not prevent Nelson from enlisting for a third time. As a private in the Medical Corps, his third attempt at service lasted a total of six weeks and ended in desertion. In March 1918, he returned to the navy. This time Nelson chose not to desert, rather he simply refused to work. The next month he was placed under observation in the Mare Island Naval Hospital.

Nelson developed an obsession for the Bible, but it did not keep him on the path of righteousness

After three weeks, as his 21st birthday approached, Nelson was transferred to the Napa State Mental Hospital.

He escaped three times from the hospital, a feat that earned him the nickname 'Houdini'. After the third success, instead of attempting to track him down, officials chose to simply let Nelson go.

He returned to San Francisco and the home of his Aunt Lillian, who helped him get janitorial work at nearby St Mary's Hospital. It was there that he met and fell in love with a maternity ward cleaning woman named Mary Martin. A 58-year-old grey-haired spinster, she must have appeared an odd match for the 22-year-old Nelson. On 15 August 1919, the couple wed. As might be anticipated, the marriage was a disaster. When not demanding sex, Nelson preferred to place his wife in the position of a maternal figure. Mary struggled to deal with these roles, while being exposed to her husband's bizarre habits. He often went days without bathing, yet changed his clothing several times a day. Many of his outfits he made from Mary's old dresses; invariably, the results were laughable.

As the relationship deteriorated, affection was replaced by jealousy. The level of Nelson's rage seemed to increase in the summer following the marriage

At the age of 18, Nelson was sentenced to two years at San Quentin for burglary. When he was released, he enlisted in the army, but soon went AWOL, before joining the US Navy – which he deserted from – and the Medical Corps

after he fell from a tree, landing on his head. He suffered a severe concussion and was hospitalized. Two days later he fled the hospital, arriving home with a turban of gauze around his head. Mary's brother encouraged her to divorce Nelson, but as a devoted Catholic she would not hear of it. Before the end of the year, they had moved in with his Aunt Lillian. Back in the house, Nelson resumed some of his old habits, among them disappearing without explanation for days on end.

In the spring of 1921, the couple relocated to Palo Alto, where they both found jobs cleaning and maintaining a private girls' school. Within days, Nelson had demonstrated to all concerned that he was unbalanced. After one particularly frightening and violent scene, witnessed by the girls eating in the school dining hall, Mary asked her husband to leave their home. The next day, Nelson returned to the school and threatened his wife. He ran off before the police arrived.

Now without a job or a home, his marriage for all intents and purposes over, Nelson was adrift. Within a few days, on 19 May 1921, he attempted to commit his first murder. The intended victim was a 12-year-old girl named Mary Summers. Nelson had gained access to the Summers' home by pretending to be a plumber sent to fix a gas leak. Not more than a few minutes into his visit, Nelson's hands were around the young girl's neck. Mary Summers' cries quickly brought her 24-year-old brother, who fought the assailant. Although he managed to flee the scene, Nelson was soon captured by police. The next month he was declared 'dangerous to be at large' and was sent to Napa State Mental Hospital. It was the very same facility from which he had escaped three times; the last time only two years earlier.

> **Nelson gained access by pretending to be a plumber. Not more than a few minutes into his visit, his hands were around the girl's neck**

Diagnosed as a psychopath, he appeared impervious to treatment. Early in his third year at the hospital, he gave warning that he would soon escape. On 23 November 1923, he did just as he'd promised, showing up in the middle of the night at his Aunt Lillian's house. She gave her nephew some clothing and, arguing that he would be tracked down to the house, urged Nelson on his way. The aunt then called the authorities. Within two days of his fourth escape, Nelson had been captured and was back at the hospital. He received a further 16 months of treatment, after which he was released. The date was 13 June 1925, nearly four years to the day since he'd tried to murder Mary Summers.

Now 29 years old, a seemingly remorseful Nelson managed to convince his wife Mary to accept him back into her life and home. Although he appeared non-violent, she still found it difficult to deal with her husband's eccentricities. It must therefore have seemed something of a blessing when he again began to roam. What she couldn't have known was that these absences often brought with them death.

The victim of Nelson's first murder was Clara Newman, a 60-year-old spinster who operated several rooming houses in the San Francisco area. On 20 February 1926, he gained entrance to one of her houses by pretending to be a prospective renter. As she showed Nelson an attic room, he attacked, strangling the landlady and raping her corpse. Ten days later, another landlady, Laura Beal, suffered a similar fate.

Newspapers picked up on the common features of the two murders and, on the basis of witness descriptions of the suspects, dubbed the murderer 'The Dark Strangler'. Several months passed without incident; both police and reporters had assumed that the murderer had left the Bay area when, on 10 June, he struck again. The victim this time was Lillian St Mary, a 63-year-old widow who had begun accepting boarders in her expansive San Francisco home. Strangled then raped, her body was found lying on a bed in one of the vacant rooms.

Two weeks later, Nelson killed and raped the proprietress of another

Nelson's first murder was Clara Newman, a 60-year-old spinster who showed him into an attic room where he attacked and strangled her, before raping her corpse. Ten days later, another landlady suffered a similar fate

rooming house, Ollie Russell. In doing so he had pulled a cord so tightly around her neck that it had torn through the skin, leaving the mattress bloody. Mrs Russell's rooming house was located in Santa Barbara, 540 kilometres south of San Francisco. It soon became apparent to authorities that the Dark Strangler was on the move.

On 16 August, Nelson murdered Mary Nisbet who, with her husband, owned a small apartment building. Two months later, the body of a youngish divorcee, Beata Whithers, was discovered stuffed into a trunk in the attic of a boarding house in Portland, Oregon. The very next day, a 59-year-old landlady named Virginia Grant was found behind the basement furnace of one of her buildings. Two days later, the body of yet another landlady, Mabel Fluke, was discovered.

As the city of Portland recoiled in horror, some in San Francisco maintained that the Dark Strangler still walked among them. It seemed that any crime involving strangulation was being blamed on the mysterious killer. In fact, Nelson did return to San Francisco, and on 18 November murdered a housebound widow. It would be his final killing in the city of his birth.

Six days later, Nelson was in Seattle, 1,300 kilometres to the north, where he killed a moneyed woman by the name of Florence Fithian Monks. Other murders followed: Blanche Myers of Portland, Mrs John Brerard of Council Bluffs, Iowa, and Bonnie Pace of Kansas City, Missouri. Perhaps the most inhumane of all Nelson's murders was discovered on 28 December when Marius Harpin returned from work to his Kansas City home to find both his 28-year-old wife and his 8-month-old son strangled.

THE DEATH TOLL RISES

After lying low for several months, Nelson resumed his activities in April 1927, killing women in Philadelphia, Buffalo, Detroit and Chicago. By 4 June, the death toll had reached 20, including that of the infant Robert Harpin. All over the United States the authorities were hunting the man known through the popular press as the Dark Strangler, Jack the Strangler and the Gorilla Man. Nelson could not have escaped the accounts of his murders in the press. Perhaps he felt that his luck could not continue. Whatever the reason, on 8 June 1927, he decided to cross the international border north of Noyes, Minnesota, entering Canada at Emerson, Manitoba. Just outside the border town he was picked up hitch-hiking by a motorist bound for Winnipeg and by late afternoon had rented a room in the home of a woman named Katherine Hill. Uncharacteristically, Nelson let his new landlady be; instead of killing her, he spent a good 20 minutes talking about the Bible.

Four days later, hours before the start of what would have been her 14th birthday, the body of Lola Cowan was found beneath the bed in the room that Nelson had rented. The smell of death had led to the discovery. The girl had been dead for nearly 72 hours.

The discovery of Lola Cowan's body followed that of another of Nelson's victims, a young wife and mother named Emily Patterson, who had been found the previous evening. Winnipeg police and the Manitoba provincial police were already looking for the murderer, who they suspected was the 'Gorilla Man' responsible for the atrocities south of the border.

By the time the bodies had been found, the killer had left the city. No doubt Nelson thought he would be able to continue as he had for the previous 16 months. It took him only a couple of days to reach Regina, 570 kilometres to the west. He arrived before the discovery of the two bodies in Winnipeg. When it broke, on 13 June, the news was on the front page of every daily in western Canada, and was accompanied by a description that was all too accurate. Nelson made his way south, intending to flee into the United States and, on 15 June, was caught within 6 kilometres of the border. Nelson was placed in a jail at Killarney, Manitoba. There, the man who had four times escaped from the Napa State Mental Hospital succeeded in picking the

Dark Strangler, Jack the Strangler or Gorilla Man: whatever you called him, Earle Nelson was fated to hang for his evil crimes

two padlocks of his cell door. He managed nine more hours of freedom before being picked up.

There would be no further escapes for the Gorilla Man. Neither his wife nor his Aunt Lillian could help him this time. Both travelled to Winnipeg, where Nelson stood trial for the murders of Lola Cowan and Emily Patterson. It was hoped that their testimonies would help bolster the argument put forward by the defence that Nelson was not sane.

On 13 January 1928, he was hanged by Arthur Ellis, the pseudonym used by the Official Executioner for the Dominion of Canada. Appropriately, the official cause of death was recorded as 'death by strangulation'.

PETER KÜRTEN

'Just you wait a little while,
The nasty man in black will come.
With his little chopper,
He will chop you up!'

So begins *M*, the first sound film by the great German director Fritz Lang. The speaker is a young girl who is playing a schoolyard game. Although she is not seen again in the film, one presumes that she remains quite safe. The same cannot be said for another character, a schoolgirl named Elsie Beckmann, who soon falls victim to a serial killer of children. The murderer is portrayed by Peter Lorre, and the character he plays, Hans Beckert, is thought to have been based on a man named Peter Kürten. Lang always denied that he'd used Kürten as a model – and it must be said that there are great differences between the two, the foremost being that Kürten's crimes were so much more horrific than anything that had been portrayed on film.

Born on 26 May 1883 at Müllheim, Germany, the man who has come to be called the Vampire of Düsseldorf was the third of 13 children. Raised in poverty, as a child Kürten witnessed his alcoholic father's repeated sexual assaults on his mother and at least one of his sisters. He himself suffered through years of

'Look at all the lovely toys.' Peter Lorre with child actor Inge Landgut in Fritz Lang's early talkie M. *Lang always denied that the film was based on the murders of Peter Kürten, but there were inevitably a number of similarities*

vicious beatings by the head of the household. Kürten turned to petty crime and several times attempted to run away from home.

Late in life, Kürten claimed that as a child he had actually murdered two young friends while swimming in the Rhine, holding each under water until they drowned. He also claimed to have befriended a local dog-catcher, who taught him how to masturbate and torture the dogs they caught together. It is thought that during this period he also engaged in bestiality.

In 1894, the family moved to Düsseldorf. He continued in his petty thievery and was soon serving the first of what would be a series of 27

Kürten claimed to have murdered two childhood friends, holding them down in the Rhine until they drowned

short prison sentences. In fact, Kürten would spend most of his life incarcerated in one institution or another. While in custody he would make a point of committing minor offences in order to be placed in solitary confinement. Once alone, Kürten would dream of mass murder – he found these fantasies sexually stimulating. For a time, beginning in 1899, he lived with a masochistic prostitute who was twice his age.

On 25 May 1913, Kürten committed his first provable murder during what would otherwise have been a routine burglary. His victim, a 13-year-old girl named Khristine Klein, was strangled and sexually assaulted. She died after Kürten cut open her throat. The next day, he sat drinking in a café across the street from the murder scene, reading descriptions in the newspaper, and eavesdropping on the conversations going on about him.

In addition to murder and stealing, Kürten had for many years been committing acts of arson. It was the sight of destruction, including that of human life, which excited him to the point of climax. His 1921 marriage had no erotic appeal. He would later say that the union had been made for companionship alone.

For many years, it seems that arson and quite likely rape satisfied his desires. This changed suddenly and dramatically on 8 February 1929 when he sexually assaulted and killed an 8-year-old named Rosa Ohliger. Found the next day beneath a hedge, the body of the dead girl bore 13 stab wounds. Kürten had doused the corpse with gasoline and set it alight – an act that brought him to orgasm.

Five days later he grabbed a woman off the street and stabbed her 24 times.

Two photographs of the so-called 'Düsseldorf Vampire' in police custody. He was classified by Professor Karl Berg as a 'narcissistic psychopath' and he never showed any remorse at all over the crimes he had committed

Incredibly, she survived the assault. Kürten found that visits to the scene of the crime would stimulate him sexually.

The next victim, a 45-year-old mechanic, was killed on 18 February. Kürten had stabbed the man 20 times, including several times to the head.

There followed six months of what seems to have been inactivity, during which a mentally handicapped man named Strausberg confessed to Kürten's crimes. He was committed to an asylum.

On 21 August, Kürten resumed his attacks in dramatic fashion, stabbing three people out walking through the Düsseldorf suburb of Lierenfeld. Two

No one was safe on the streets of Düsseldorf when Peter Kürten was around. He seemed to be spurred on by his extraordinary sex drive, achieving euphoria through random acts of murder and violence

nights later, he came upon two girls, 5-year-old Gertrude Hamacher and her 14-year-old foster sister Louise Lenzen, walking home from the annual fair in the town of Flehe. Kürten asked Louise to get him some cigarettes, and sent the girl, money in hand, back to the fairground. While Louise was away, he strangled Gertrude and cut her throat. When Louise returned from the errand, she was strangled and decapitated.

The next day, he propositioned a servant girl named Gertrude Schulte. When she replied that she'd rather die than have sex with him, Kürten stabbed her, saying 'Die then'. Schulte survived and was able to provide an accurate description of her assailant.

Kürten then, inexplicably, put down his knife. His next victims were both beaten to death: a young girl named Ida Reuter in September, and another servant girl, Elizabeth Dorrer, in October. Two other women were also beaten, both with a hammer, but survived.

On 7 November, he abducted a 5-year-old girl named Gertrude Albermann. The two-day search for the

Human prey: Kürten trawled Düsseldorf for victims, and not even children were spared his murderous acts

missing girl came to an end after Kürten sent a detailed letter to a local newspaper in which the location of the girl's body was revealed. She had been stabbed 35 times.

It would prove to be Kürten's final murder.

More hammer attacks, none of them fatal, took place during the months of February and March 1930. Then, on 14 May, he encountered Maria Budlick, yet another servant girl. She had travelled from Köln to Düsseldorf in search of work. On the railway platform she met a man who offered to show her the way to the local hostel. As Budlick walked with the man she was reminded of newspaper stories she'd read about murders in Düsseldorf and refused to go any further. An argument ensued, only to be broken up by the arrival of another man: Peter Kürten.

Budlick accompanied the man she thought of as her rescuer to his home, where she was fed. Kürten then led the girl into the local woods and raped her.

Although he had been certain that Budlick would not be able to lead police to his home, within days Kürten realized he'd been wrong. Finding he was under police surveillance, he confessed all his crimes to his wife and urged her to turn him in for reward money. After some reluctance – she had proposed a suicide pact – Kürten's wife agreed. He was arrested on 24 May.

While in prison awaiting trial, Kürten relayed details of his life and crimes to German psychologist Karl Berg. With great clarity, the murderer dictated vivid accounts of a total of 79 crimes, which he numbered and presented in chronological order. Berg would later use the interviews as the foundation for his 1932 book on Kürten entitled *Der Sadist*.

In April 1931, Kürten was put on trial for nine murders and seven attempted murders. He pleaded not guilty, stating that his confession was only an attempt to secure a lucrative reward for his wife. However, as the trial progressed, he changed his plea to guilty and, as he had with Berg, began to talk openly and with great detail about his crimes.

M leaves the viewer with an ambiguous ending. Hans Beckert, the Lorre character, is about to receive his sentence, but the film finishes before it is pronounced. Will Beckert be sentenced to death or will he be found insane? Peter Kürten's fate is much more clear. Found guilty, on the morning of 2 July 1931, he was executed in Köln by guillotine. His final wish was that he might remain alive long enough to hear the blood flowing out of his severed head.

CARL PANZRAM

As the moment of his execution approached, when serial killer Carl Panzram was asked whether he had any last words, he is reported to have turned to his executioner and said: 'Hurry it up, you Hoosier bastard! I could kill ten men while you're fooling around!' It was probably not much of an exaggeration.

Much of what we know about Panzram comes from his autobiography, published 40 years after his death. It is a well-written and articulate account of his life; not at all what one would expect from someone with limited formal education. The man who would come to murder dozens was born to a Prussian immigrant couple on 28 June 1891 on a Minnesota farm near the Canadian border. He and his six siblings were raised in poverty, a situation made worse when his father deserted the family. This shameful act took place when Carl Panzram was 7 years old. A year later the boy was arrested for the very adult crime of being drunk and disorderly. He was soon committing burglary, and at the age of 11 was sent to the Minnesota State Training School, a reform institution. Panzram's claims, made late in life, that he was beaten and sexually abused, are probably true. That he also committed his first murder there, the victim being a 12-year-old boy, has not been verified. In July 1905, he burnt one of the school's buildings to the ground. Evidently, he wasn't a suspect in the destruction, as he was released just a few months later.

He enrolled in another school, but was soon in conflict with one of the teachers. The dispute was elevated to such a point that Panzram brought a handgun to class, intending to murder the instructor in front of his fellow

Carl Panzram was gang-raped and went on to forcibly sodomize more than a thousand boys and men

students. The scheme collapsed when the gun fell to the floor during a struggle. He left the school and the family farm, and started 'riding the rails'. Any feeling of freedom the 14-year-old might have felt in this transient lifestyle probably came to an end when he was gang-raped by four men. For the rest of his 39 years, Panzram was enraged by the pain and humiliation he had suffered through the incident. As part of some warped idea of revenge, he went on to forcibly sodomize more than a thousand boys and men.

Mere months after having left the Minnesota State Training School, Panzram was again in reform school, again for having committed burglary.

He soon escaped with another inmate named Jimmie Benson. They remained together for a time, moving around the American midwest, causing havoc, burgling houses and stealing from churches before setting them on fire.

After they split up, Panzram joined the United States Army. It was a strange choice of profession, one for which he was ill suited. During his brief stint in service, he was charged with insubordination, jailed numerous times for petty offences and, ultimately, was found guilty on three counts of larceny. Panzram received a dishonourable discharge and on 20 April 1908 was sentenced to three years of hard labour at the United States Disciplinary Barracks at Fort Leavenworth in Kansas.

In prison, the 16-year-old Panzram was beaten and chained to a 50-pound metal ball which he was made to carry. He dreamed of escape, but found it impossible. It was only after serving his three-year sentence that he finally got out. Panzram returned to his old transient lifestyle, moving through Kansas, Texas, California, Oregon, Washington, Utah and Idaho. He committed burglary, arson, robbery and rape. In his autobiography, Panzram writes that he spent all his spare change on bullets and for fun would take shots at farmers' windows and livestock.

Prisoners at Fort Leavenworth Penitentiary march towards the mess hall for dinner. Panzram did three years hard labour here, during which time he was chained to a 50-pound metal ball and frequently beaten

Panzram fenced goods in the Lower East Side in the shadow of Brooklyn Bridge and bought himself a yacht on the proceeds. Then he started sailing the East River and breaking into the yachts of the wealthy

Another story involves a railway policeman whom Panzram raped at gunpoint. He forced two hobos to witness the act and then recreate it themselves.

He was arrested many times and served a number of sentences under a variety of assumed names. After his second incarceration and escape from Oregon State Prison, Panzram made his way to the east coast. Ending up in New Haven, Connecticut in the summer of 1920, Panzram burgled the home of former United States president William H. Taft, the man who had once signed the paper sentencing him to three years in prison at Fort Leavenworth.

The haul from the Taft mansion far exceeded previous burglaries. After fencing the goods in Manhattan's Lower East Side, Panzram bought a yacht. He then sailed the East River, breaking into the yachts of the wealthy moored along his route. He took to hiring unemployed sailors as deckhands. In the evenings, he would drug his crew, sodomize them, shoot each in the head with a pistol stolen from the Taft house and throw their bodies overboard. After about three weeks, Panzram's routine came to an end when his yacht was caught in an August gale and sank. He swam to shore with two sailors, whom he never saw again.

Following a six-month sentence for burglary and possession of a loaded gun, Panzram stowed away on a ship bound for Angola. While in the employ of the Sinclair Oil Company he sodomized and murdered a young boy. He later hired six locals to act as guides and assist in a crocodile hunting expedition. Once downriver, with crocodiles in sight, he shot all six and fed the men to the beasts. After travelling along the Congo River and robbing farmers on the Gold Coast, he made his way back across the Atlantic.

Following his return to the United States, Panzram continued where he left off, committing robbery, burglary and sodomy. These 'routine' crimes were punctuated by the murders of three boys; each was raped before being killed.

On 26 August 1923, Panzram broke into the Larchmont, New York, train depot and was going through the stored baggage when he was confronted by a policeman. He was sentenced to five years in prison, most of which were served at Clinton Prison in upstate New York. True to character, Panzram made no attempt to become a model prisoner. During his first months at Clinton he tried to firebomb the workshops, clubbed one of the guards on the back of the head and, of course, attempted to escape. This final act had consequences with which he would struggle for the rest of his life.

The incident began when Panzram failed in his attempt to climb a prison wall. He fell nearly ten metres, landing on a concrete step. Though his ankles and legs were broken and his spine severely injured, he received no medical attention for 14 months. The months of agony Panzram endured intensified his hatred and he began to draw up elaborate plans to kill on a mass scale. One scheme involved blowing up a railway tunnel, then releasing poison gas into the area of the wreck.

When he was finally released from Clinton, in July 1928, Panzram emerged a crippled man. However, his diminished capacity did nothing to prevent his return to crime. During the first two weeks of freedom, he averaged approximately one burglary each day. More seriously, on 26 July 1928, he strangled a man during a robbery in Philadelphia. By August, Panzram was again in custody. Perhaps realizing that he would never again leave prison, he confessed to 22 murders, including those of two of the three boys in the summer of 1923.

On 12 November, he went on trial for burglary and housebreaking. Acting in his own defence, he used the courtroom as a stage from which to scare the jury and threaten witnesses. By the end of the day he had been found guilty on all counts and was sentenced to a total of 25 years in prison.

On 1 February 1929, he arrived at the United States Penitentiary at Leavenworth, Kansas. It was an area of the country he knew well; 20 years earlier he had served time at the nearby military prison. Standing before his new warden on that first day, Panzram warned, 'I'll kill the first man that bothers me.' True to his word, on 20 June 1929, Panzram took an iron bar and brought it down with force on the head of Robert Warnke, his supervisor in the prison laundry. When the other prisoners attempted to escape, Panzram began chasing them around the room, breaking bones.

He was tried for Warnke's murder on 14 April 1930. Again, he undertook his own defence, smugly challenging the prosecutor to find him guilty. It wasn't a difficult challenge. When the judge sentenced Panzram to hang, he was threatened by the condemned man.

On 5 September 1930, Panzram was hanged. Many organizations had worked to prevent the execution, much to Panzram's annoyance. Nine months before his death, he wrote to one such organization, the Society for the Abolishment of Capital Punishment: 'The only thanks you and your kind will ever get from me for your efforts on my behalf is that I wish you all had one neck and that I had my hands on it.'

Panzram's sadism knew no bounds. In Angola, he hired six locals to act as guides and assist in a crocodile hunting expedition. Once downriver, with the crocodiles in sight, he shot all six and fed the men to the beasts

THE LUST KILLERS

In the 1960s a new term, 'lust killers', was coined to cover what appeared to be a series of psychopathic sexual predators. Some of these men mutilated sexual organs, performed acts of necrophilia and positioned the bodies of their victims in sexually suggestive poses, while others committed none of these crimes at all. However, all the lust killers had one thing in common: the attainment of sexual gratification through murder.

HARVEY GLATMAN

As a child, Harvey Glatman was taunted in the schoolyard. His large ears and buck-teeth earned him nicknames like 'Weasel' and 'Chipmunk'. As he grew older his looks did not improve. His only recorded date was with a beautiful woman, whom he killed.

Born in New York in 1927, Glatman was a peculiar child. This observation, first made when he was a baby, was shared by his parents. Alternately giggling or crying, his emotional reactions seemed to have no connection to his environment. He appeared to display no interest in his toys, or anything else for that matter. In private, however, he was cultivating an obsession with things sexual, particularly acts involving sado-masochistic behaviour. Decades later, on the witness stand, Glatman's mother would trace her son's fascination back to the age of 4, when she had caught him pulling a piece of string he had tied around his penis.

In school Glatman proved to be studious, preferring the classroom to the playground, where he would be obliged to interact with other children. He was frightened of girls his age who often joined the boys in making fun of his looks. The schoolyard taunts began afresh, in a different location, after the family left the Bronx for a new life in Denver, Colorado.

At a very early age, he discovered autoerotic asphyxia, and would use ropes in self-induced strangulation while masturbating. When Glatman was 11 years old, his parents discovered their son's pastime, and sought the advice of a medical doctor. The result was that he took greater caution not to be caught in the future.

As he entered his teenage years, he developed a bad case of acne, which only contributed to his isolation from others in his age group.

Harvey Glatman was an unusual child, alternately giggling and crying for no apparent reason

In public an accomplished student, he began to secretly break into private homes. Glatman's motivation was not material, but the thrill derived from a risky act. Usually, but not always, he would steal a souvenir with which to remember his adventure. A stolen handgun was among his most prized possessions.

Eventually, the break-ins evolved into a more dangerous and violent act. Glatman took to prowling the streets looking for attractive women. Once an appealing subject had been spotted, she would be followed home. Later that evening Glatman would return, break into the house, tie up his victim and gag her mouth. He would then fondle the women, often through their clothes; they would never be fully undressed.

NIGHTLY ACTIVITIES

Glatman's parents, believing an improbable story that their son had joined in extracurricular activities with schoolmates, were not suspicious of his nightly absences.

On 18 May 1945, carrying a handgun and some rope, he was caught by police while attempting to break into a woman's apartment. Taken into custody, he confessed to several burglaries, none of which involved bondage and molestation. While awaiting trial for burglary, he committed a much more serious crime in abducting an attractive woman named Noreen Laurel. After tying her up, he drove 50 kilometres into Sunshine Canyon, where she was fondled. Later, he drove his captive back to Denver, where she was released. Laurel went directly to the police and identified her abductor from a picture in a book of mugshots. Glatman was again arrested. That November he was sentenced to one year in Colorado State Prison.

This model student also seemed a model inmate. Eight months into the sentence, he was paroled. Accompanied by his mother, who was well aware of her son's reputation in Colorado, Glatman relocated to Yonkers, New York. He obtained a job as a television repairman, a trade he had learnt while incarcerated.

Glatman waited until his mother left before resuming the lifestyle that had caused so much trouble. Well aware that, for a parolee, possession of a handgun could lead to an extremely long prison sentence, he purchased a realistic-looking cap gun.

On 17 August, a mere three weeks after leaving the Colorado State Prison, Glatman pulled the cap gun on a young couple. The incident departed from that of a typical mugging when he produced a rope and bound the legs of the male. Pressing the cap gun against her stomach, Glatman was fondling the female's breasts, when her boyfriend managed to escape his bonds. He grabbed the assailant from behind, but was stabbed in the shoulder. Glatman escaped and was soon on the move to Albany.

Five days later, he assaulted an off-duty nurse, but she started to fight back

Glatman was transferred from Elmira Reformatory to notorious Sing Sing in upstate New York after being diagnosed with a psychopathic personality. He proved a model prisoner and gained maximum parole

as he was tying her wrists. Again, Glatman ran away. He then mugged two young women. Within days, Glatman was caught. In October, having received a five-to-ten-year sentence, he was living at New York's Elmira Reformatory. Upon reaching the age of 21, he was transferred to the famous Sing Sing Correctional Facility, but not before having been diagnosed as having a psychopathic personality.

Again, Glatman proved to be an exemplary inmate, so much so that he was granted parole after having served just over half of his five-year minimum sentence. Obliged to stay in his parents' custody, he returned to Denver, where he began the first of what would be a long series of jobs.

In September 1956, Glatman was released from parole. No longer required to live in Denver, he drove around the westernmost states. After four months, he settled in Los Angeles. Glatman set himself up as a television repairman and returned to photography, a hobby he'd had as a teenager. In the evenings he took advantage of local modelling agencies, which offered girls and women willing to pose semi-nude or nude.

On the afternoon of 1 August 1957, he brought a 19-year-old model named Judy Dull to his apartment. Told that the photographs had been commissioned for a true crime magazine, Dull was bound and gagged. Once she was secure, Glatman threatened the model with a gun, taking pictures all the while. From time to time he would untie Dull's legs, rape her, and again replace the ropes. As the day drew to a close, he announced that the time had come to let her go.

With her wrists tied, Dull was led to Glatman's car and made to sit inside. The television repairman drove for two hours, pointing his gun at Dull, until he had passed Thousand Palms, 200 kilometres away from Los Angeles. According to Glatman, while pretending to release the model he used the ropes deftly to break her neck. He then arranged her body for a few more photographs.

Glatman's next victim was a 24-year-old named Shirley Ann Bridgeford, whom he met through the Patty Sullivan Lonely Hearts Club. Calling himself George Williams, on 7 March 1958 he arrived at her home for what was meant to be a first date; there he was introduced to several of Bridgeford's relatives. He was supposed to take his date out to dinner, followed by square dancing. They did share a meal, but afterwards Glatman drove with Bridgeford into the Vallecito Mountains. After raping her, Glatman used flashbulbs to take photographs of his victim in the dark countryside. He then waited for the sun to come up so that he could take even more pictures. Eventually, he strangled Bridgeford with a rope and took additional photographs of her corpse.

Four months later, he returned to the Vallecito Mountains with a model named Ruth Mercado. He had already raped the 24-year-old in her Los Angeles apartment. There, in the wilderness, Glatman raped her again, had her pose for photographs and strangled her with a rope. Other models were much more lucky – they were hired, photographed and returned home unaware that they had been in the company of a rapist and murderer. He had begun to use Diane Studio, an agency that was more respectable and pricier than his former choices. On 27 October, he hired Lorraine Vigil, the agency's newest model.

From the time he picked her up, at eight in the evening, Vigil was careful around Glatman. Caution turned to suspicion when Glatman changed the location of their shooting. When she confronted him verbally, Glatman pulled over to the side of the road, took out a handgun and told her to hold out her arms. He attempted to tie her wrists, but she fought back, holding on to the barrel of the gun. It fired through Vigil's skirt, the bullet skimming her thigh. She then kicked open the door and,

Glatman's photograph of Shirley Ann Bridgeford before he raped and strangled her, then dumped her body

holding the gun, fell out on to the gravel shoulder of the road. Glatman was grabbing at her sweater, trying to pull Vigil back inside when he was interrupted by the headlights of a passing police car.

Whimpering, Glatman was arrested and taken to Orange County, where under interrogation, he confessed to the murders of Judy Dull, Shirley Ann Bridgeford and Ruth Mercado. He surely knew it was only a matter of time before the authorities came upon his collection of their photographs.

Glatman's trial was a short one. At its centre was the playing of a four-hour taped confession in which the accused described in detail and without emotion each of the three murders. On 15 December 1958, Glatman was condemned to death.

During the nine-month wait until his execution date, Glatman was held at San Quentin State Prison. He was separated from the rest of the inmates; his home was a cell that would a decade later hold Charles Manson.

On 18 September 1959, Glatman was taken to the prison gas chamber. After he was strapped to a chair, the door was sealed and sodium cyanide pellets were dropped. He took just under nine minutes to die.

THE BOSTON STRANGLER

Albert DeSalvo's father, Frank DeSalvo, was a Newfoundland fisherman who had found work in Boston as a machinist. A sadistic monster, he would beat his wife and six children on a regular basis. Fists, belts and pipes were used for the smallest of indiscretions. As a boy, Albert DeSalvo witnessed his father beat his mother until all her teeth had fallen out. Then, as she lay on the floor in pain, Frank DeSalvo took his wife's hands and proceeded to break each finger in turn. His father would repeatedly pick up prostitutes, bring them into the family home and have intercourse with them in front of his children. Forever being arrested for not supporting his family, Frank DeSalvo once attempted to relieve the financial burden by selling Albert and his four sisters to a farmer for nine dollars.

Many serial killers suffered as children, and Albert DeSalvo's early years appear to have been exceptionally horrific. Might his tragic childhood have influenced his future as a serial killer, as some have claimed? Or might there be something else in play? After all, none of DeSalvo's siblings became murderers. Perhaps, though, these are the wrong questions. A better one might be: Was Albert DeSalvo really the Boston Strangler?

The murders attributed to the Boston Strangler begin on 14 June 1962 with that of Anna Slesers. The body of this 55-year-old Latvian seamstress was discovered in the early evening when her son arrived at her apartment,

January 1968 and Albert DeSalvo is escorted into Middlesex County Superior Court, Cambridge, Massachusetts: DeSalvo's father once attempted to sell Albert and his four young sisters to a farmer for nine dollars

intending to take her to church. He thought initially that his mother had committed suicide; indeed the fear had led him to break down her door when she hadn't responded to his knocking. However, the police quickly came to a different conclusion. Slesers' body was found, half-clothed in a robe, lying on the bathroom floor. It was obvious that she had been sexually assaulted and then killed. Death had been brought about by the cord of the robe, which had been tightly knotted around her neck. Slesers' apartment appeared to have been burgled, though many valuables had been overlooked. The police theorized that the murderer's original plan had been to steal from the apartment, but had come across Slesers, who he then molested.

Their supposition would be questioned when, 16 days later, a 68-year-old named Nina Nichols was found dead in her apartment. As with the Latvian seamstress, Nichols had been sexually assaulted. She had been killed by a nylon stocking tied around her neck. The victim's apartment bore signs of a burglary, but again most valuables had been left behind. Oddly the murderer appeared to have gone through Nichols' mail and her address book.

Later that day, the body of another woman was found in the Boston suburb of Lynn, some 25 kilometres to the north. The victim, 65-year-old Helen Blake, had been sexually assaulted and strangled with a nylon stocking. Her apartment had been ransacked.

After the discovery of two bodies in a single day, the Boston Police Department issued a warning to all women in the area, advising them to be wary of strangers and to ensure every door was locked. All detectives in the force were transferred to the case, police holidays were postponed, and a thorough investigation of all known sex offenders was undertaken.

However, these efforts did nothing to prevent the Boston Strangler, as he had come to be known, from striking again.

On 19 August, a 75-year-old widow, Ida Irga, was murdered in the city's West End. Efforts had been made to arrange the corpse in something reminiscent of an obstetrical examination, which faced the door so as to be the first thing seen upon entering. Although a pillowcase was knotted about her neck, Irga had died from manual strangulation.

Her body lay undiscovered for two days. Before it was found, the Strangler had already murdered another woman, a 67-year-old nurse named Jane Sullivan, on the other side of the city. Her body was found in the apartment bathtub, a nylon stocking knotted around her neck. But the corpse had been lying in the August heat for ten days and was in such a state of decomposition that police were unable to determine whether or not the victim had been sexually assaulted. Nonetheless, police estimated that Ida Irga and Jane Sullivan had been murdered within 24 hours of one another.

Many studying the Boston Strangler describe his murders as having taken place in two waves. The first begins with the 14 June 1962 murder of Anna

Police file photos of eight of the victims of the Boston Strangler: an insatiable sexual appetite combined with an appalling childhood seems to have turned DeSalvo into a sadistic and rapacious monster, but was he the Strangler?

Slesers, and ends less than ten weeks later with Jane Sullivan's killing. What followed was more than three months of inactivity. When the Boston Strangler resumed, his preference in victims appeared to have switched from older to younger women.

The first victim of the second wave was Sophie Clark, an attractive 20-year-old medical student, murdered just a few blocks away from what had been Anna Slesers' apartment. She had been strangled using a nylon stocking. A half slip had also been placed around her neck. This time there was no evidence of sexual assault, perhaps due to the fact she was menstruating. Semen was found close to her body on the living room rug.

The Strangler's next victim, 23-year-old Patricia Bissette, was murdered on the morning of 31 December 1962. Her body was found lying face up in bed, covers drawn over her neck. When removed, they revealed that Bissette had been strangled with several stockings and a blouse, knotted and interwoven. She had also been raped.

As the first months of 1963 passed without incident, hopes began to rise that the Strangler would never strike again. However, on 8 May, the body of

23-year-old graduate student Beverly Samans was discovered in her Boston apartment. Although two scarves and a nylon stocking had been knotted around her neck, they had played no role in her death. Rather Samans had been stabbed 17 times, including four wounds to the throat.

There followed another quiet period. When the Strangler resumed, he appeared to have returned to his original victim type. The body of Evelyn Corbin, a 58-year-old divorcee, was found in her bed. She had been sexually assaulted and strangled with two stockings tied around her neck.

On 25 November, the date on which the body of John F. Kennedy was being interred at Arlington National Cemetery, the killer struck again. His victim, 23-year-old Joann Graff, was beaten, raped and strangled with two nylon stockings and a black leotard.

MACABRE MESSAGE

On 4 January 1964, a 19-year-old named Mary Sullivan was sexually assaulted and killed. Her body was left sitting upright in bed, dressed only in a bra and open blouse. Around Sullivan's neck was a rope the Strangler had made consisting of a nylon stocking and two scarves. He had left a message for the authorities – a greeting card propped up against the corpse's left foot, it read 'Happy New Year!'

If those attempting to catch the Boston Strangler saw anything happy in the New Year, it lay in the fact that he appeared to commit no further murders. There seemed to be no explanation for the inactivity. Then, in March 1965, they were provided with an answer when Albert DeSalvo, an inmate of the Massachusetts Correctional Institution, confessed to the murders. It appeared that they had unknowingly locked up the Boston Strangler months before.

Born 3 November 1931, Albert Henry DeSalvo had progressed from a ghastly childhood to become a career criminal. He once stated that it had been his father who had taught him how to steal. DeSalvo's first arrest took place in November 1943, just after his 12th birthday, when he was charged with assault and battery with intent to commit robbery. He was sent to the Lyman School for Boys, the first reform school in the United States. DeSalvo's education at Lyman did nothing to curb his criminal behaviour.

Despite his shameful record, at the age of 17 he managed to join the United States Army. He was sent to Europe, where he met and married a German woman whom he brought back to the United States. He was then posted to Fort Hamilton, New York, and Fort Dix, New Jersey. It was while serving at the second of the two bases that DeSalvo was arrested for having molested a 9-year-old girl. He escaped prosecution only because the girl's mother didn't want to press charges.

His sex drive was described as insatiable. He demanded sex from his wife six or more times a day. When she rebuffed his advances, DeSalvo would fly into a rage and accuse her of being frigid. Their relationship soured further after their first child was born with a pelvic disease. Fearing further children with birth defects, DeSalvo's wife all but curtailed their sex life.

When he confessed to the murders that had been attributed to the Boston Strangler, DeSalvo was in prison for a string of seemingly unrelated assaults. The last, occurring on 27 October 1964, had led directly to his arrest. On that morning, DeSalvo broke into the apartment of a sleeping 20-year-old university student. After she was awoken, DeSalvo proceeded to tie the woman up and then fondle her.

The victim's description led police to identify the assailant. When DeSalvo's photograph was published in Boston area newspapers, other women identified him as the man who had assaulted them.

DeSalvo was not a suspect in any of the strangling cases. His confession was made to fellow prisoner George Nassar, who reported it to F. Lee Bailey, his attorney. Bailey, in turn, took on DeSalvo as a client and represented him as he repeated his confession to the police. All who heard the prisoner speak were impressed by the accuracy with which he described the crime scenes. Though there were some inconsistencies, DeSalvo provided details that had not been made available to the public. To the tally of 11 murders attributed to the Strangler,

State troopers hold back a crowd of 2,000 curious onlookers outside the Lynn Street police station after Albert DeSalvo was captured in a West Lynn uniform store 30 hours after his escape from prison

DeSalvo added two others. The first victim, a 68-year-old woman named Mary Brown, had been found bludgeoned, stabbed and strangled in her home in Lawrence on 6 March 1963. The second woman, also elderly, had been so frightened that she had died of a heart attack before he could strangle her.

However, not one piece of physical evidence was found at any of the crime scenes that could substantiate his story. Despite the 2,000-page transcript of his confession, DeSalvo stood trial only for the unrelated crimes of robbery and sexual assaults. In January 1967, he was sentenced to life in prison.

The next month he and two fellow inmates escaped from Bridgewater State Hospital, setting in motion a full-scale manhunt. DeSalvo left behind a note stating the escape was intended as a means of focusing attention on the conditions in the hospital and his own situation. He gave himself up the next day and was transferred to the maximum security Walpole State Prison.

On 25 November 1973, DeSalvo was found murdered in the prison infirmary. His killer (or killers) has never been identified.

> Despite the 2,000-page transcript of his confession, DeSalvo stood trial only for unrelated crimes of robbery and sexual assaults

There have always been serious doubts as to whether DeSalvo was the Boston Strangler. At the time of his confession, it seems all who had known him, including police officers with whom DeSalvo had long histories, believed he was incapable of committing the crimes.

Confusing the issue was the belief among many in the police department that there was no Boston Strangler, rather that the 11 murders were committed by two or more individuals. Today, sceptics of the idea that there was a single strangler point out that the victims came from different age and ethnic groups, and that there were very different patterns to the murders. Moreover, killing by strangulation in the Boston area did not end with Mary Sullivan, the supposed final victim.

And then, there was the matter of evidence. There was no physical evidence linking DeSalvo to any of the crime scenes. No witnesses could place him at or near any of the sites.

Why would DeSalvo admit to these horrible crimes if he didn't actually commit them? One theory rests on DeSalvo's realization that he would likely be incarcerated for the rest of his life for the crimes of burglary and assault. Looking for a means with which to support his wife and children, he entered into an ill-fated scheme in which George Nassar would receive a significant reward for turning in DeSalvo as the Boston Strangler. Accordingly, the two men would have split the proceeds.

DeSalvo once told F. Lee Bailey that he hoped to be able to provide for his family by writing a book on his crimes. He was murdered before ever being able to carry out the plan.

RICHARD SPECK

Richard Speck believed that he'd been born to raise hell. Indeed, as a teenager he had had those very words tattooed on his arm. It was neither a young man's folly, nor an idle boast.

Richard Franklin Speck was born 6 December 1941 in Kirkwood, Illinois, a small village of a few hundred people located midway between Chicago and Kansas City. The seventh of eight children, he was very close to his father, Benjamin Speck. His young life was thrown into turmoil at the age of 6 when his father died. His mother relocated with some of the children, Richard included, to Fair Park, Texas, where she married a man named Carl Lindberg. Speck watched as his mother, a religious woman with no tolerance for alcohol in the home, adapted to marriage with a drunken, violent man who had a history with the police. Speck came to hate his stepfather with the same passion he had shown in loving his father.

In Texas, he was a poor student and demonstrated little interest in school. The eighth grade was the last he managed to complete. Before his 12th birthday he had begun to drink, as both an escape and a means of countering severe headaches brought on, most likely, by a series of head injuries.

Entering adolescence, Speck was arrested for the first time. His offence, trespassing, would be joined by charges of burglary and stabbing as he progressed towards adulthood.

In November 1962, he married a woman named Shirley Malone. The next year, the couple had a baby daughter. But his approach to the role of father was in stark contrast to that of Benjamin Speck. Convictions on theft, cheque fraud and aggravated assault charges meant that he spent much of the marriage in prison. In January 1966, Speck's wife filed for divorce. She would claim that on at least one occasion he had raped her at knifepoint.

Shortly thereafter, Speck was charged in a stabbing and burglary. Incredibly, he was let go after paying a fine of ten dollars. With the support of his sister, he returned to the area of Illinois in which he had spent his early years.

On 2 April, an elderly local woman, Mrs Virgil Harris, was attacked, bound and raped. Nine days later, a barmaid named May Kay Pierce was found dead behind Frank's Place, Speck's tavern of choice. He was questioned for the second crime, but became sick during the interrogation and was let go.

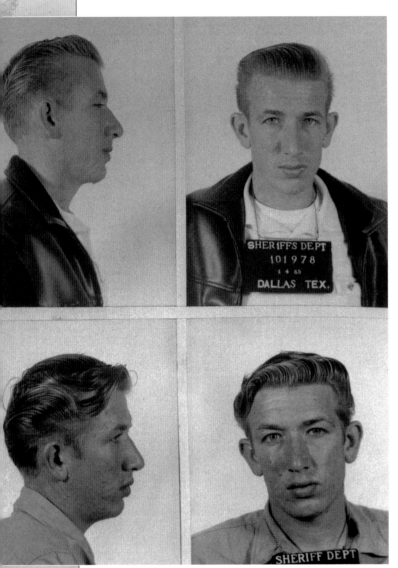

Mugshots of Richard Speck released by the Dallas County Sheriff Department from 1965 (top) and 1961 (bottom)

The eight nurses who were subject to Richard Speck's ghastly attentions

Although he promised to return on 19 April, he never did. Local police tracked him to a hotel, but found he had run out just a few hours earlier. Left behind in Speck's room they found a radio and jewellery belonging to Mrs Harris.

Speck seemed to have disappeared; in actual fact he had found work on a ship on the Great Lakes. As he travelled, bodies seemed to appear in his wake. He was soon wanted for questioning about the disappearances of three females and the murders of four others.

At approximately 11 o'clock on the evening of 14 July 1966, a student nurse named Cora Amurao answered a knocking at the door to a townhouse dormitory in South Chicago. She was met by Speck holding a handgun. Grabbing her by the arm, he made his way through the townhouse threatening the women with his gun, until they'd all been gathered in one of the bedrooms. There were six of them. Another student nurse, Gloria Davy, arrived home from a date and had the misfortune of stumbling into the scene.

Speck would later claim that his original intention was simply to rob the women. Indeed, each was made to give him money from their purses. However, he was soon ripping sheets from one of the bunk beds, using the strips to tie each woman's wrists and ankles.

He had completed this task when another two students, Suzanne Farris and Mary Ann Jordan, arrived home. When they came upon Speck and the bound women, they tried to flee the townhouse. Speck ran after the pair. They were forced into another of the bedrooms. He stabbed Jordan three times, including once in the eye. Farris was strangled with a white nurse's stocking and stabbed 18 times in the chest and neck. They were the first of eight women who would die.

Although he would later claim to have been high on alcohol and drugs, Speck spent the next several hours methodically removing the women from the room, either individually or in pairs. He would take each to another bedroom, where they would be beaten, raped and stabbed. Cora Amurao managed to escape this fate

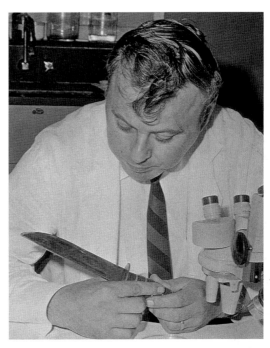

Crime lab technician Louis Vitullo holds the knife sold for $1 by Speck hours after the slayings of the eight student nurses

by hiding under one of the beds and pressing herself as tightly as possible against the wall. Speck simply lost track of the number of women he had bound. It later came out that he had known eight women lived in the dormitory, but was unaware that there had been one visitor. That visitor happened to be Amurao.

After Speck left the dormitory, Amurao remained hidden, not daring to come out from under the bed until five the next morning. She ran to the balcony and began screaming, 'They're all dead! All my friends are dead! Oh God, I'm the only one alive!'

With a survivor on their hands, police moved quickly in identifying Speck. However, not all police officers had been alerted to the identity of the killer. Two days after the murder, the police were called to a rundown hotel to investigate a complaint that a man named Stayton had a gun in his room. Awakened by the cops, Stayton gave his name as Richard Speck and explained the gun by saying that it belonged to a prostitute he'd picked up the night before. Satisfied, the police left.

Drunk on beer and cheap wine, Speck kept moving through the low-rent areas of Chicago, always ahead of the police. However, by 19 July his name and photograph were all over the front pages of the local newspapers. Speck bought these papers and a bottle of cheap wine, which he drank after returning to the cheap hotel room he'd rented. He then smashed the bottle and used the broken glass to slice open his wrist and inner elbow. He was discovered by the desk clerk, and taken by ambulance to Cook County Hospital. It was LeRoy Smith, the doctor who worked to save Speck's life, who identified the killer. He had read all about the wanted man and recognized the 'BORN TO RAISE HELL' tattoo from a newspaper description.

While being treated, Speck told Smith that he had committed the murders of the eight student nurses. However, it was a confession made under the influence of sedatives, and so could not be used in court. When he had recovered from his suicide attempt, Speck maintained that he had no memory of the evening in the dormitory.

Speck's trial began on 3 April 1967. The evidence presented appeared overwhelming. At the centre of those testifying was the survivor Cora Amurao. When asked whether she could identify the man who had murdered her friends, she rose from her seat, unlatched the witness box door, walked across the courtroom and stood pointing before Speck, saying, 'This is the man.'

Two weeks later, when asked for their decision, it took the jury just 49 minutes to declare Speck guilty and to recommend the death penalty. Speck was sentenced to death on 5 June, a conviction that set in motion over five years of legal manoeuvrings. The penultimate decision, made on 21 November 1972, sentenced Speck to eight consecutive terms of between 50 and 150 years. The following year, this was reduced to a new statutory maximum of 300 years.

He was incarcerated at Stateville Correctional Center, a maximum security prison in Crest Hill, Illinois. Though he preferred solitary pastimes, such as stamp collecting, Speck was anything but a model prisoner. Most of his infractions involved drugs and bootleg alcohol. He sought and was denied parole on six different applications, the last being in 1990.

Speck died of a heart attack on 5 December 1991, the day before what would have been his 50th birthday. An autopsy performed on his brain revealed gross abnormalities. However, further examination and study was curtailed after samples disappeared.

Speck's unclaimed body was eventually cremated. A service was held, attended only by the county coroner, a deputy, a newspaper columnist and a pastoral worker. His ashes were spread in an undisclosed location.

The death of Richard Speck was a news story for a day or two; some media outlets provided summaries of his awful crimes. Then, just as Speck slowly began to fade from modern memory, in May 1996 a videotape surfaced. Believed to have been shot two years before his death, it features a bizarre-looking Speck with pendulous breasts, wearing blue silk panties. He is shown taking drugs and having sex. But more shocking than the visual images are Speck's words, answers to questions posed by another inmate. He describes the process and strength required in strangling someone to death. When asked about the deaths of the eight nurses, he responds, 'It just wasn't their night.'

Controversy followed. Some advocates of the death penalty used the tapes to support their cause. Others stated that it was obvious Speck was being forced by other inmates into the acts, and argued for penal reform.

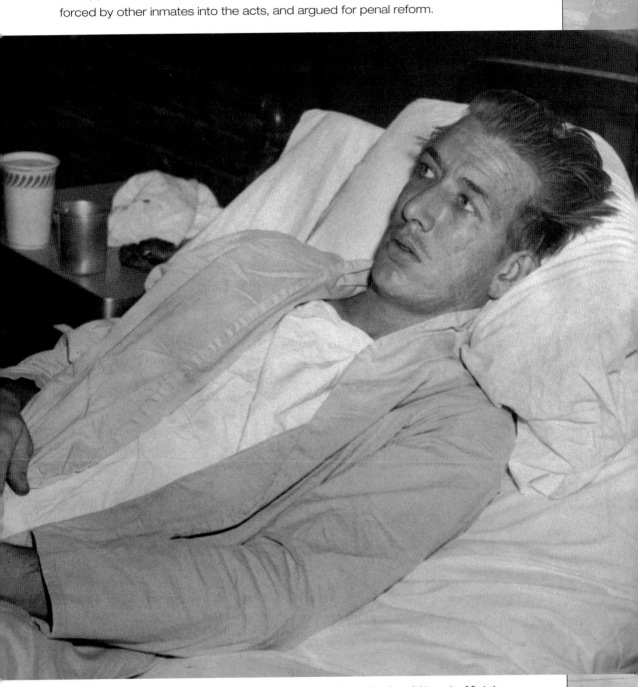

'It just wasn't their night.' Speck contemplates his future after being arraigned on eight counts of first-degree murder. He was sentenced to eight consecutive terms of 50 to 150 years, commuted to a maximum of 300 years

EDMUND KEMPER

It is sometimes claimed that serial killers want to be caught. Increasing sloppiness, risk-taking and taunting yet revealing letters sent to the authorities are often cited as proof. Ultimately, this is nothing more than speculation; we cannot really know. However, it can be said with certainty that Edmund Kemper, the Co-Ed Killer, wanted to be caught, and that's down to the simple fact that he actually turned himself in.

Edmund Emil Kemper III was born on 18 December 1948 in Burbank, California, the home of the Walt Disney Company and Warner Brothers. An only son, he had one older and one younger sister. Kemper was named after his father, with whom he was extremely close. In 1957, his parents divorced, and his mother moved with the children to Helena, Montana. There, nearly 2,000 kilometres away from his father, Kemper suffered his mother's emotional abuse. She would often lock him in the basement, thinking that he would molest his sisters. While still a child he began to torture and kill animals, and used his sisters' dolls in acting out aberrant sexual fantasies and situations. On more than one occasion, his younger sister found that her dolls had been decapitated. In a favourite childhood game Kemper would dream of his own execution, enlisting one of his sisters to lead him to a pretend electric chair.

At the age of 13 he ran away from home and made his way back to California. His father, who had remarried, was somewhat less than pleased to see him. It was during the trip that Kemper learned he had a stepbrother – a boy who had replaced him in his father's affections. He was sent back to Montana, where he was equally unwelcome.

As a 14-year-old, he was sent to live with his paternal grandparents, Maude and Edmund Kemper, on their 17-acre ranch in North Fork, California. Already considerably more than six feet tall, he was an awkward boy,

Ed Kemper was born in Burbank, Ca. At 13, he ran away from home in Montana and made his way back to California

both physically and socially. Despite his height, he was easily bullied. According to Kemper, his grandmother was another in a list of tormentors.

On the afternoon of 27 August 1964, the two argued and, taking the rifle given to him by his grandfather the previous Christmas, Kemper shot his grandmother once in the head and twice in the back. It was an impulsive act. His grandfather arrived home and was shot as he got out of his car. Kemper would later say that he killed his grandfather to spare the old man the discovery of his dead wife, killed by his grandson.

After phoning his mother to tell her what he had done, Kemper called the local police and waited on the porch for their arrival. In custody he was diagnosed as having paranoid schizophrenia and sent to the Atascadero State Hospital for the Criminally Insane.

From an early age, Kemper dreamt of his own execution, enlisting his sister to lead him to a pretend electric chair

On his 21st birthday, 18 December 1969, against the wishes of several psychologists, he was released into his mother's care. She had moved back to California during her son's incarceration, and was now living in Santa Cruz, a rapidly growing beach town to the south of San Francisco. Kemper attended community college and received high marks. He became friendly with various members of the Santa Cruz Police Department. For a time he planned on becoming an officer, a dream that ended when he learned he was too tall. Now standing 6 feet, 9 inches, and weighing nearly 300 pounds (over 20 stone), Kemper was an imposing figure.

He worked at a number of jobs before settling into a position as a labourer with the California Division of Highways, an occupation that had some relationship to his subsequent crimes. Kemper wasn't good with money, but he managed to save enough to move out of his mother's home and share an apartment with a roommate. He also purchased a motorcycle, which played a part in two separate accidents. As a result of one of these, Kemper received a settlement of $15,000. He used this money to buy a yellow Ford Galaxie, and began to cruise the area along the Pacific coast in search of female hitch-hikers. By his own estimation, he generously provided rides to approximately 150

At 6 foot 9, even the police looked up to Ed Kemper, but he was no gentle giant. Here he is being arraigned in 1973

young women and girls, all the while slowly gathering items of sinister purpose in his trunk: knives, handcuffs, a blanket and plastic bags.

On 7 May 1972, he picked up his first victims, Mary Ann Pesce and Anita Luchessa, who were hitch-hiking 270 kilometres from Fresno to Stanford University. At first the girls felt themselves lucky, as Kemper told them he would drive all the way to Stanford. However, he soon drove off the highway and on to a deserted dirt road. There he stopped, killed both girls, and drove back to the highway with their bodies in his car boot. In a scene reminiscent of a movie cliché, Kemper was almost caught when, as he drove back to his apartment, the police pulled him over and issued a warning for a broken tail light.

Kemper arrived at his apartment to find that his roommate was out. He carried in both bodies, laid them on the floor of his bedroom and began to dissect them, taking photographs to mark his progress. He later admitted that he'd had sex with various severed parts. He disposed of the girls' bodies in the mountains, burying that of Pesce in a shallow grave which he marked in order to find it on future visits.

During the next four months he continued to give lifts to women, often engaging in conversations about an unknown man who was murdering female hitch-hikers.

On 14 September, he raped and killed Aiko Koo, a 15-year-old girl who had decided to hitch-hike after becoming tired of waiting for a bus. She, too, was taken to the apartment and dissected.

The next day Kemper went before two psychiatrists, a requirement of his parole. As a result of the interview, it was immediately concluded that he was no longer a danger. Later, he disposed of Koo's body parts outside Boulder Creek.

The following January and February, Kemper killed three more women, two of whom he picked up at the University of California's Santa Cruz campus,

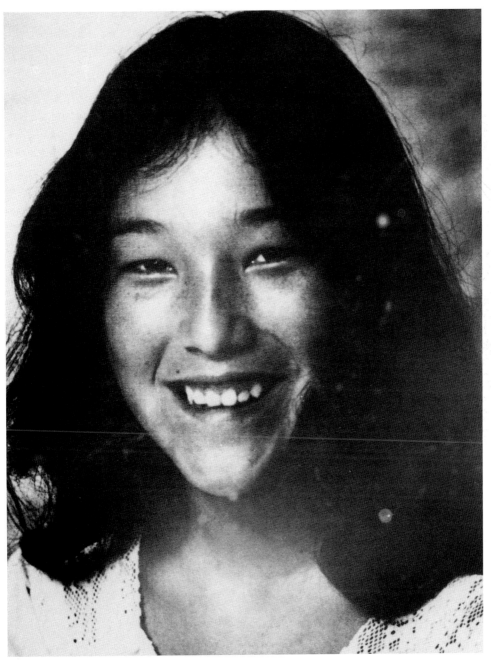

Aiko Koo, who decided to hitch-hike rather than wait for her bus: after accepting a lift from Kemper, she was raped and murdered. The next day psychiatrists came to the conclusion her killer was no longer a danger

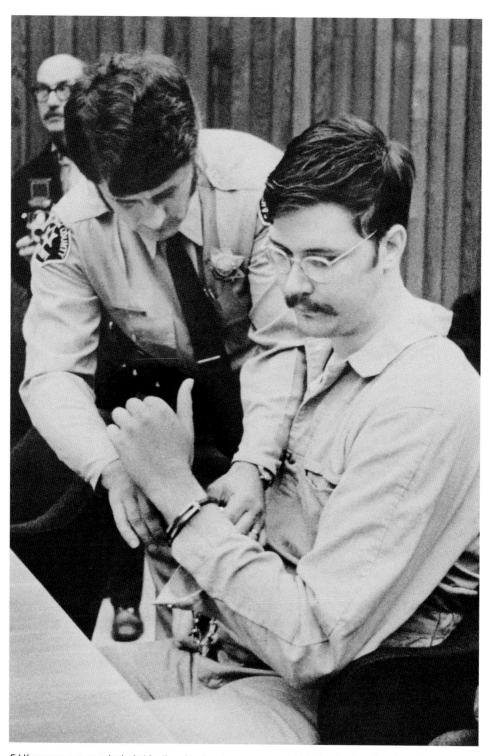

Ed Kemper was once asked what he thought when he saw a young girl in the street, and replied, 'One side of me says I'd like to talk to her and date her. The other side of me says I wonder how her head would look on a stick?'

where his mother was employed. These same two women he dismembered and beheaded in his mother's home.

On 21 April 1973, Good Friday, Kemper killed his mother with a pick hammer as she slept. After decapitating her, he sexually assaulted the corpse. The head he placed on the mantelpiece, where he used it as a dart board. He then invited over one of his mother's female friends, Sally Hallett, whom he strangled and beheaded.

On Easter Sunday, he drove off eastward in Hallett's car, listening for news reports of the murders he had committed on the radio. After driving approximately 2,400 kilometres without hearing a word on his crimes, Kemper pulled off the road. From a phone booth in Pueblo, Colorado, he phoned his old friends at the Santa Cruz Police Department and confessed to the murder of his mother, her friend and the six female hitch-hikers. However, the officer who took the call, knowing Kemper, did not think him at all capable of the crimes, and considered the call a practical joke made in poor taste. It took several further phone calls to convince the Santa Cruz police that a visit to Mrs Kemper's house might be warranted.

On 7 May 1973, Kemper was charged with eight counts of first-degree murder. While awaiting trial, he twice attempted suicide. The trial began on 23 October and lasted less than three weeks. Kemper's plea of not guilty by reason of insanity was countered by three prosecution psychiatrists who declared him to be sane. In the end, he was found guilty on all eight counts.

He asked to be sentenced to death, but his childhood fantasy was denied. Kemper is currently serving a sentence of life imprisonment in the California State Medical Corrections Facility.

JERRY BRUDOS

The mind of the serial killer seems such a mystery; explanations of their crimes are beyond the realm of the easy answer. Incredibly, some observers have blamed the troubled life and horrific crimes of Jerry Brudos, Oregon's worst serial killer, on the void created by the absence of a mother's love.

Jerome Henry Brudos was born on 31 January 1939 in South Dakota, the third child in a family that already included two boys. He would later say that his mother had so hoped for a daughter that the birth of yet another son was a great disappointment. Raised by a mother who viewed him with scorn, Brudos grew up with the knowledge that at least one of his parents thought he had been born the wrong sex. He sought approval and friendship from other females, but often found himself ignored and very much alone. As he matured, so too did his attraction to women's shoes and lingerie. The roots of Brudos' fetishes are quite deep and, unnervingly, can be traced back to a very early age. As a 5-year-old, he uncovered a pair of stiletto-heeled shoes at a local dump, and later was caught wearing them by his mother. Her strong and violent reaction, which included the destruction of his treasure, may very well have served to fuel Brudos' interest in women's footwear as something forbidden. At the same age, he was caught stealing the shoes of his kindergarten teacher.

By the age of 17, Brudos' desire for the feminine had taken a more serious turn. He abducted a 17-year-old girl at knifepoint, and led her to a local hillside in which he had excavated a large hole. Once there, Brudos beat the girl and forced her to remove her clothing. The assault was interrupted by an elderly couple out for a stroll and he was arrested.

As a result, Brudos spent nine months in the psychiatric ward at the Oregon State Hospital, where he openly discussed his fantasies with the attending doctors. He explained that the hillside dugout had been intended as a place to keep girls he wanted to use as sex slaves. One of his more disturbing fantasies concerned dumping women into freezers so that he might later use their stiff bodies in creating sexually explicit poses and scenes. Amazingly, as Brudos provided doctors with details of his various dreams and desires, he was permitted to attend his high school classes. Ultimately, these same mental health practitioners determined that their teenaged patient was suffering from nothing more than a difficulty in adjusting to adolescence. Despite the abduction, the beating and the hole he'd created for sex slaves, the future serial killer was considered a person not prone to violence.

After high school, Brudos enlisted in the military, but was soon discharged as an undesirable recruit. He became an electronics technician and, in 1961, married a shy 17-year-old, five years his junior. At the beginning of their marriage, Brudos insisted that his bride remain naked when at home. Exactly how long this rule remained in place is unknown – it may have lasted until the birth of his children, or perhaps the arrival of his mother. Whatever the answer, there was another rule that remained in place. All were forbidden to enter certain areas of the house – rooms in which Brudos indulged his sexual fantasies. And yet, as the years passed, Brudos' wife caught glimpses of his secret life: a paperweight in the shape of a breast, photographs of nude women. On one occasion he appeared before her in women's underwear; garments probably obtained by breaking into other people's houses. During at least one of these break-ins, Brudos encountered a woman and raped her.

On 26 January 1968, he committed what is thought to have been his first murder. The victim was Linda Slawson, a 19-year-old who was trying to raise money for university by selling encyclopaedias door to door. Brudos lured the young woman into his workshop, where she was clubbed on the head, then strangled. All this took place while, at Brudos' encouragement, the rest of the family sat eating at a local fast food restaurant. Over the next few days, he dressed, photographed and sexually violated the corpse. Eventually, he disposed of Slawson's body by throwing it off a bridge into the Willamette

River – but not before amputating one of her feet, which he kept and used to model his collection of women's shoes. When the severed foot had deteriorated to a point at which Brudos no longer found it to be of use, it too was thrown in the river.

Eleven months later to the day, he murdered again. The second victim was Jan Whitney, whom he encountered on a roadside after her car had broken down. Brudos took her to his house, saying that she would be able to wait with his wife, while he returned to repair the car. Instead, he strangled Whitney, sexually violating the corpse before carrying it to his workshop. Again, he took photographs and dressed the corpse in his collection of women's clothing. For several days he left the body hanging from the ceiling.

Despite his actions, and the fact that his crimes were taking place within a house shared with his wife, his children and, of course, his mother, Brudos seemed to think that there was no way he would be caught. It was then that a rather bizarre accident took place. A car struck his house, damaging the structure to such an extent that passers-by could easily view the inside. Before the police could investigate the

Jerry Brudos strangled Jan Whitney in his house – then he left her body hanging from the ceiling

interior of the house, Brudos took down Whitney's body and hid it in a small structure on his property.

When it was time to dispose of Whitney's body, Brudos cut off her right breast. He had hoped to use it as a mould in making paperweights like the one he had purchased, but was unsuccessful in his attempts.

On 27 March 1969, his next murder victim, Karen Sprinker, was abducted at gunpoint and taken to his home. Unlike the previous women he'd killed, Brudos raped Sprinker before killing her. She was forced to model various items from his collection of women's clothing, and was eventually hanged. He cut off both breasts, dressed the corpse in a longline bra, and stuffed the cups.

In late April, using a fake police badge and the threat of a charge for shoplifting, Brudos abducted Linda Salee, his final victim. She was bound in his workshop, waiting while he had dinner, before being sexually assaulted and strangled. Brudos later claimed that she was being raped at the moment of death.

The Willamette River where Brudos dumped the body of Linda Slawson. He lured her into his workshop, clubbed her on the head, then strangled her, before dressing, photographing and sexually violating the corpse

The disappearances of all four women remained complete mysteries to the authorities; all appeared to have simply vanished. Then, in May, a man out fishing found decomposing human remains floating in the Long Tom River. After the police arrived, more remains were discovered bound to a car transmission box. The body was identified as that of Linda Salee.

The speed with which the authorities zeroed in on Brudos is truly impressive. Among the clues used in identifying the killer was the manner in which copper wire had been used to bind Salee's body; an unusual technique that indicated someone with training as an electrician.

On 30 May, he was arrested. Just as he had when he was a patient at the psychiatric ward of the Oregon State Hospital, Brudos openly discussed his sexual fantasies. Indeed, while under interrogation, he appeared to seize upon the opportunity presented to share his secret dreams with others. There was no expression of remorse for his victims. What little sympathy Brudos had was directed towards his wife and children – but most certainly not to his mother.

For his crimes, Brudos received three life sentences. He died of natural causes on 28 March 2006. At the time of his death, Brudos was the longest-serving inmate at Oregon State Penitentiary.

O.J. SIMPSON

O.J. Simpson's life is the quintessential American rags-to-riches story gone wrong. As a sporting idol, he was almost universally loved. But he turned out to have feet of clay. Simpson was wildly successful in his football career. His exploits in college were rewarded in 1968 with the Heisman trophy, the Maxwell Award and the Walter Camp Award, three of the most respected awards in college football.

Orenthal James, 'O.J.', Simpson was nicknamed 'The Juice'. He was a phenomenally gifted footballer with a great record in the game, not bad for a kid who had rickets in childhood which left him bow-legged and pigeon-toed

Nicole and O.J. were a 'dramatic, fractious, mutually obsessed couple before they married, after they married, after they divorced, and after they reconciled, at the fraying edge of which reconciliation the murder occurred'

His professional career was even more successful. He was drafted first overall by the Buffalo Bills in 1969. His career lasted until 1978 and during that time he put up over 11,000 yards rushing – at the time placing him second on the NFL's all-time rushing list. Throughout his career, he shattered records: in 1973 he became the fastest player to gain 1,000 rushing yards in a season, and he remains the only player to have rushed for over 2,000 yards in a 14-game season.

After his retirement from football he began a successful career in the film industry, acting in the television series *Roots* and a number of films including *The Towering Inferno* and the *Naked Gun* trilogy. He also spent time working as a commentator for *Monday Night Football* and broadcast NFL games on NBC.

But what of his personal life? Simpson married Marguerite L. Whitley in June 1967 at the age of 19. They had three children together, Arnelle, Jason and Aaren. In 1977 Simpson met Nicole Brown, a waitress at a nightclub, and they began dating, though he was still married to Marguerite. Simpson and Marguerite divorced in March 1979. Just five months later, Simpson's youngest child, Aaren, tragically drowned in the family swimming pool.

Simpson and Brown married in February 1985 and had two children, Sydney and Justin. This relationship was a troubled one, too. It lasted seven years before Brown had had enough of Simpson's violent behaviour.

But far worse was to come.

> Detectives discovered a white Ford Bronco smeared with blood outside his house in Brentwood... Simpson was nowhere to be found

MATCHING GLOVES

On 12 June 1994 Nicole Brown and one of her friends, Ron Goldman, were found stabbed to death at Brown's home in Los Angeles. Brown had been stabbed several times in the head and neck. The first officer on the scene, Robert Riske, found a single bloody glove nearby.

When the detectives came to inform Simpson that his ex-wife had been murdered, they discovered a white Ford Bronco smeared with blood outside his house in Brentwood. Simpson was nowhere to be found. The vehicle was impounded by police. A second bloody glove, matching the one found at the murder scene, was found inside the house. This was more than enough evidence for the LAPD to issue an arrest warrant, but Simpson seemed to have vanished off the face of the Earth.

At 11 a.m. on 17 June 1994 Simpson was scheduled to surrender. At 5:51 pm a call was made to 911 from his cell phone. The call was traced to a white Ford

Bronco – Simpson's car, or so they thought. A car chase began immediately. Strangely enough this was not actually Simpson's vehicle, though he was hidden in the back. It was owned by A.C. Cowling, a childhood friend who idolized Simpson and copied everything he did. So when O.J. came to him in desperation, he was only too happy to help. The pursuit, lasting about 90 minutes, was televised live and interrupted coverage of the NBA Finals. Eventually his former college coach at USC, John McKay, went on the air and encouraged Simpson to give himself up. Ninety-five million Americans watched the saga of Simpson's capture unfold.

The trial that ensued was one of the most infamous in American history. A grand jury had to be dismissed because it was feared that the extensive media coverage might have prejudiced their opinions. Simpson hired an all-star team of lawyers for his defence. Led by Robert Shapiro, the team included Jonnie Cochran, Robert Kardashian, Carl E. Douglas and others, and two attorneys who specialized in DNA evidence – Barry Sheck and Peter Neufeld.

Trial by television

The trial was held in downtown Los Angeles, well away from where the murder occurred. This was just one of many controversial decisions. It resulted in a jury pool drawn from a more working-class, ethnically diverse area than would have been found in Santa Monica. The trial was televised for 134 days, beginning on 24 January 1995. In the end, the prosecution decided

The Ford Bronco involved in the 90-minute car chase was owned by O.J.'s friend A.C. Cowling; ninety-five million Americans watched the saga unfold

The Simpson trial was headline news across the world and rapidly turned into a three-ring media circus; televised throughout by Court TV, the defendant was accused of killing his wife in a jealous rage

only to ask for life imprisonment rather than the death penalty.

Prosecutor Christopher Darden painted Simpson as a violent man who had killed his ex-wife in a fit of uncontrollable jealousy and passion. He used a 911 call by Nicole Brown from 1989, when she was still married to Simpson, to support his case. Brown displayed fear that Simpson would harm her and Simpson could be heard shouting in the background.

A succession of expert witnesses was called, giving their opinions on every aspect of the case, to place Simpson at the scene of the crime. Reams and reams of circumstantial evidence existed: strands of hair consistent with Simpson's were found on Goldman's body; the bloody glove in his house; the bloody shoeprints; and Brown's blood was found on socks in his bedroom. Even without a murder weapon and with no witnesses, Darden thought he had a strong case.

But it relied heavily on Simpson's history of spousal abuse. His defence lawyers argued convincingly that most domestic abusers did not go on to commit murder.

Simpson's story changed with the wind. First he claimed he was asleep at the time of the murders. Then he was alone in his house packing for his trip to Chicago. A testimony from Rosa Lopez claimed she had seen his car parked outside his house at the time of the murders, but her account fell apart under cross-examination. The defence came up with a surprising strategy: they claimed Simpson was not physically capable of the murders.

Goldman was a fit young man. Simpson, though an ex-football player, now had chronic arthritis and scars on his knees from the injuries he had received during his football career. The real change in momentum came when

O.J. Simpson tries on a glove in court allegedly used in the murders of Nicole Brown Simpson and Ron Goldman, 15 June 1995

Cochran was able to persuade the court that there was reasonable doubt regarding the DNA evidence presented. The most damning evidence now had to be disregarded.

DIVIDED NATION

On 3 October 1995 Simpson was acquitted. Reaction to the verdict divided along racial lines. African-Americans mostly believed justice had been served by the not guilty verdict, while white Americans tended to believe Simpson was guilty. The Brown and Goldman families were not satisfied. They filed a civil lawsuit against Simpson and on 4 February 1997 the jury found Simpson responsible for the two deaths. They received $33.5 million in damages.

At the trial, numerous bits of information were kept from the jury. A local resident, Jill Shively, testified that she saw Simpson speeding away from Nicole's house on the night of the murders. Another witness claimed to have sold a knife similar to the murder weapon to Simpson a few weeks earlier. These two witnesses chose to sell their stories to the press. A woman's shelter, Sojourn, had received a call from Brown just four days before her murder confirming her fear of her ex-husband, whom she believed was stalking her.

The prosecution chose not to use the evidence as they believed

Passion took O.J. Simpson to the very top in everything he did, but did it finally drive him to murder?

the judge would dismiss it as hearsay. And the most damning piece of evidence could not be used even if the prosecution had wished to. Rosey Grier had visited Simpson at the LA County Jail days after the murder. Simpson had told him, so he alleged, he 'didn't mean to do it'. But Judge Ito ruled the evidence was hearsay and could not be used in court.

No one else has ever been charged with the murders. It seems possible that O.J. Simpson was still responsible for the deaths of Nicole Brown and Ron Goldman. Certainly the civil trial would suggest so. A book written by Simpson in 2006 entitled *If I Did It* provides a hypothetical confession by him. But a documentary by the BBC in 2000, *OJ: The True Untold Story,* suggested that the prosecution had planted evidence which pointed to Simpson and had too easily ignored other possible suspects, including Simpson's elder son, Jason, and individuals in the drug trade.

Whatever the truth of the matter, in 2007 O.J. Simpson was convicted of multiple felonies after a robbery at the Palace Station Hotel, Las Vegas – involving some sporting memorabilia that Simpson claimed had been stolen from him – and sentenced to 33 years in prison for kidnapping, burglary and armed robbery. He began his sentence at the Lovelock Correctional Center in Nevada in December 2009.

On his way to a wedding, Simpson and five accomplices drove to the Palace Station hotel in Vegas and demanded that memorabilia dealer Alfred Beardsley hand over items that Simpson claimed were his

THE RISE OF THE SERIAL KILLER

As the 20th century entered its final decades, the incidence of serial murder dramatically increased, particularly in the United States. In 1984, President Reagan described the perpetrators as 'repeat killers' and the FBI made the startling announcement that there were approximately 35 such murderers active in the country at any given time. Before Reagan's administration left office, a new term, 'serial killers', was in common usage.

JOHN WAYNE GACY

John Wayne Gacy devoted a great deal of time and effort to the betterment of his community. He served on the board of the Catholic Inter-Club Council and was commanding captain of the Chicago Civil Defense. In his immediate neigbourhood, he organized elaborate, themed block parties, at which he would entertain as Pogo the Clown. Active within the Democratic Party, he once had his photograph taken with future-First Lady Rosalynn Carter. Gacy hoped that one day he would make a name for himself by running for political office – but as Christmas 1978 approached, he became famous for entirely different reasons.

Born in Chicago to Irish parents on St Patrick's Day 1942, Gacy was the first son in the family. While growing up on the city's north side, he was bullied by his father, the man after whom he had been named, who would accuse him of being a sissy. Despite this, Gacy junior looked up to his father with something amounting to hero-worship. He seemed entirely capable of turning a blind eye to the old man's alcoholism and violent outbursts.

Among John Gacy Sr's many complaints was that his namesake was a sickly child. At 11 the young Gacy was hit on the head with a swing. For the next five years, he suffered from recurring blackouts. The condition was left undiagnosed until the age of 16 when a blood clot was discovered on his brain. It was later dissolved with the use of medication. The following year, Gacy was hospitalized with a heart ailment, the cause of which was never determined. Though he never once suffered a heart attack, Gacy complained about the pain for the rest of his life.

Conscientious and hard-working, as a boy Gacy held several after-school jobs. Although he wasn't a particularly bad student, he moved from high school to high school before dropping out in his senior year. After graduation, he left home for Las Vegas, where he was certain well-paying jobs awaited. Gacy ended up as a janitor in a funeral home, saving desperately for a return ticket to Chicago. This bitter lesson taught him the value of education. Upon his return, Gacy enrolled in a business college. He soon learned he had a talent for sales and before long was manager of a men's clothing store in Springfield, Illinois. Although his health again began to suffer, he became active in a number of civic organizations, including the Jaycees (Junior Chamber of Commerce), who named him 'Man of the Year'.

In September 1964, he married a co-worker, Marlynn Myers. The couple relocated to Waterloo, Iowa, nearly 500 kilometres west of Chicago, where Gacy managed three Kentucky Fried Chicken restaurants owned by his new father-in-law. The couple had two children. For a time, it seemed that Gacy was well on his way to establishing himself as one of the pillars of the community. However, rumours began to circulate that he was making sexual advances to his young employees.

In May 1968 he was arrested after he'd raped one of his workers, a 16-year-old named Mark Miller. The teenager claimed that while visiting the Gacy home a year earlier, he had been tied up and forcibly sodomized. Gacy maintained that members of the Jaycees were framing him and that the sexual encounter had been consensual.

As he waited for his case to come to trial, he hired a man named Dwight Anderson to beat up Miller. The victim was taken to a wooded area and sprayed with mace, but managed to escape after breaking Anderson's nose. Miller later identified his assailant who, in turn, revealed that he had been provided with $310 to perform the beating. In the end, Gacy pleaded guilty and was handed a ten-year sentence.

While he was behind bars, Gacy's wife divorced him – he never saw her or his children again. Equally damaging, his father died, fully aware of the crime of which his son had been convicted.

Gacy was a model inmate, and on 18 June 1970 managed to obtain parole after having served only 18 months. He returned to Chicago and lived with his mother. With her help, in 1971 he bought a bungalow in Norwood Park Township, just outside Chicago, and quickly set out to establish himself in the

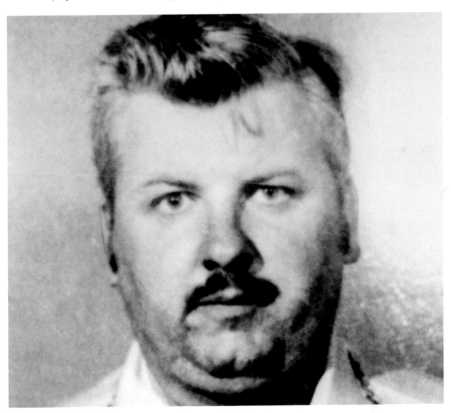

John Wayne Gacy was a pillar of the community, organizing themed block parties and entertaining as Pogo the Clown, but his sexual transgressions began to take on more and more sinister forms

community. By autumn, Gacy was no longer under parole. He had made many friends in the neighbourhood, none of whom were aware of his criminal record. Christmas was spent with a local family whom he had invited to share in the festivities. It may have appeared that Gacy had been reformed – and yet less than two months into the New Year he was charged with disorderly conduct after having forced a boy at a bus terminal into sexual acts. The case was dismissed when the accuser failed to show at the court proceedings.

On 1 June 1972, Gacy remarried. His second bride, Carol Hoff, was a divorcee with two daughters; they had known each other since high school. Carol was well aware of her husband's past incarceration, but shared in the opinion that he was a reformed man and joined him in his active social life.

Together they helped host and organize street parties, including one event that was attended by over 300 guests. She watched as her husband toured children's wards in hospitals, dressed in a clown costume of his own design.

In 1974, Gacy established a painting and decorating business. His employees were invariably teenage boys. He was particularly drawn to those who were fair-haired and well-built. As in Iowa, rumours again began to circulate concerning Gacy and his employees. When Carol Gacy began finding gay pornography in their house, her husband nonchalantly explained that he simply preferred adolescent boys to adult women. The couple were divorced in March 1976.

Incredibly, neither criminal record nor rumour prevented Gacy from having political aspirations. He began volunteering for a number of community projects and offered to clean the local offices of the Democratic Party. Though he rose slowly through the ranks,

Gacy began painting on Death Row. This far from benign image was auctioned after his execution

rumours continued to grow concerning his private life.

All began to be revealed following the disappearance of a 15-year-old boy named Robert Piest. On 12 December 1978, Piest had emerged from the pharmacy where he had a part-time job. He told his mother, who had come to pick him up, that he would be right back after speaking with a contractor

> **The crawl space under Gacy's house had become so crowded that he was forced to dispose of some of the bodies in the Des Plaines River**

who was looking to hire him. He never returned.

Piest's mother remembered the name of the contractor and several hours later a police officer was at Gacy's front door. Gacy told the man that he was unable to leave the house as there had been a recent death in the family and he had phone calls to make. He later appeared at the police station and provided a statement to the effect that he knew nothing of the disappearance.

After a background check revealed that Gacy had once been convicted of sodomy with a minor, a search warrant was issued for his property. Hundreds of objects were removed from Gacy's house and three vehicles were seized. Items were shown to belong to Piest and several other missing boys. An excavation of the crawl space under Gacy's house revealed the remains of 27 boys and young men. Gacy later said that the crawl space had become so crowded that he was forced to dispose of some of his victims' bodies in the Des Plaines River.

Fully aware of what had been discovered at his home, on 22 December Gacy confessed to killing at least 30 people – it was clear that he had lost count. He said that many of the victims had been invited to his home. The first murder had taken place in January 1972, 18 months after he'd been released from prison. He'd killed for the second time in January 1974, while still living with his second wife. After their separation, the murders had taken place with increasing frequency. In most cases, Gacy admitted, he would invite boys and young men into his home, where he would offer to show them a magic trick using fake handcuffs which were part of his clown act. The handcuffs would prove to be all too real. Gacy would then chloroform and rape his victim. After many hours of torture, death would come through either strangulation or asphyxiation.

Most of the victims were young male prostitutes or teenage runaways, but Gacy had also been so reckless as to prey upon boys he'd hired through his own contracting company. At least four boys went missing while in his employ, yet the local police failed to recognize the significance of this commonality.

The body count grows as investigators carry another corpse from Gacy's house. He was convicted of 33 murders and sentenced to death, but had to wait 14 years before the penalty could be carried out

Although some corpses were so badly decomposed that they could not be identified, it is thought that his youngest victim was just less than ten years old. Nine unidentified corpses were buried under separate headstones bearing the words 'We Are Remembered'.

Gradually, it became apparent that there had been other victims; young men who had not been killed, but had been set free by the murderer. Among these was Jeffrey Ringall, whom Gacy had enticed into his car with the promise of marijuana. Not long after they began sharing their first joint, Ringall had a chloroform-doused cloth shoved in his face and lost consciousness. Ringall spent the rest of the car journey drifting in and out of consciousness, but didn't truly regain his senses until he was in Gacy's home.

By this point Gacy had removed all his clothes and was standing naked in front of him demonstrating a number of sexual toys. During the next several hours, Ringall was sodomized, tortured and drugged. He awoke the next morning, fully clothed, in Chicago's Lincoln Park. The next six days were spent in hospital. When reporting the assault, Ringall was told by the police that it was doubtful they would ever be able to identify his assailant.

Ringall was fortunate in that his story had been believed by the police. Another of Gacy's victims had been raped, urinated on, dunked repeatedly in a bathtub and forced to play Russian roulette. His captor, who was later identified as Gacy, correctly predicted that the police would not believe the story of the assault.

During his trial, beginning on 6 February 1980, Gacy attempted to withdraw his confession, and plead not guilty by reason of insanity. As if to support the claim, Gacy tried to joke with the jury, saying that he was guilty of nothing more than 'running a cemetery without a licence'. He also claimed to suffer from multiple-personality disorder, and said that an alter-ego named Jack was responsible for the murders.

On 13 March 1980, Gacy was convicted of 33 murders and sentenced to death. He was transferred to Menard Correctional Center, where he was placed on Death Row. As he waited through 14 years of appeals, Gacy took up oil painting. His favourite subject was portraits of clowns, which he painted and sold at great profit. At a 1994 exhibition at the Tatou Gallery in Beverly Hills, California, Gacy's portraits sold for as much as $20,000.

Gacy was executed on 10 May 1994 at Stateville Penitentiary in Illinois. When asked whether he had any last words, Gacy is reported to have snarled, 'Kiss my ass.' His death, by lethal injection, was botched. As the execution began, the chemicals solidified and the IV tube that led into the condemned man's arm had to be replaced. As he died, Gacy struggled against his bonds. The entire procedure took 18 minutes, nearly four times as long as had been intended.

TED BUNDY

An intelligent, charming, good-looking law student, who already had a degree in psychology, Ted Bundy seemed destined for a brilliant future. Some in the Republican party saw him as a potential future governor of the state of Washington, and yet he ended up being sentenced to death in the electric chair.

Bundy was born on 24 November 1946 at the Elizabeth Lund Home for Unwed Mothers in Burlington, Vermont. The identity of his father has always been a matter of speculation. Bundy's birth certificate is at odds with the name provided by his mother, Louise Cowell. There is some evidence pointing to incest – that Bundy was fathered by his grandfather. As an infant he was adopted by his grandparents, and grew up believing his mother to be his older sister. It wasn't until his university years that Bundy would learn the truth of the relationship.

His earliest years were spent in Philadelphia, after which he and his 'sister' moved to live with relatives in Tacoma, Washington. The year after their relocation, when he was four, Louise met a navy veteran named Johnny Culpepper Bundy at a church singles' night. Within months they married and Johnny adopted his bride's 'brother'.

The Bundy family quickly grew to five children; as the eldest, Ted spent much of his free time babysitting. Despite this contact, he remained emotionally detached from the rest of the family, feeling that they were beneath him.

Bundy was an excellent student. Though an active Methodist, serving as vice-president of the Methodist Youth Fellowship, he remained shy and introverted throughout his teenage years. Bundy's participation in the Church is also at odds with his criminal activity. He had started shoplifting while in high school, and progressed to stealing skis and forging lift tickets. He was twice arrested as a juvenile.

Handsome and articulate, he appeared to be a generous young man. While attending the University of Washington, he gave his time to the Seattle Crisis Clinic on a suicide prevention helpline. One of his co-volunteers, a young Ann Rule, would go on to write *The Stranger Beside Me*, the finest and most famous biography of the serial killer.

In the summer of 1969, Bundy visited Vermont, where he finally learned the truth about his parentage. The news served to create a greater distance between himself and the Bundy clan.

He returned to the University of Washington, and became a psychology

Ted Bundy was brought up to be an active Methodist, but grew up 'emotionally detached', a condition not helped by the revelation that his older sister was his mother. Some Republicans saw him as a potential governor of Washington

Handsome and articulate, Bundy appeared to be a generous young man, but few got a glimpse behind the mask he wore each day – and those that did often regretted it. Starting with petty crime, Bundy worked his way up to murder

major. It was during this year that he met a young divorcee. The two entered into a relationship that would last some seven years.

In 1972, Bundy graduated with honours and soon began working for the Republican party. During a trip to California in the summer of 1973, he also resumed dating another woman, a former girlfriend from university. Though he continued to date the first woman, he proposed marriage to the second. He ended the engagement after two weeks, and later revealed that the engagement had been made so as to hurt his fiancée when rejecting her. Within weeks he would begin the first of two strings of murderous attacks.

Shortly after midnight on 4 January 1974, Bundy gained access to the basement bedroom of an 18-year-old student at the University of Washington. He took a metal rod from her bed frame, bludgeoned her as she slept and sexually assaulted her. Discovered by her roommates the next morning, she survived the attack, but suffered permanent brain damage.

On the evening of 31 January, he broke into the room of another University of Washington student, 19-year-old Lynda Ann Healy. She was knocked unconscious, dressed, wrapped in a bed sheet, and carried away, her body eventually discovered a year later. On 12 March, Bundy kidnapped and murdered Donna Gail Manson, a 19-year-old student at Evergreen State College in Olympia, Washington. On April 17, 18-year-old Susan Rancourt disappeared from the campus of Central Washington State College in Ellensburg. Having procured victims from three different Washington state institutions of higher learning, Bundy moved his operation south to Oregon State University in Covalis, from which he abducted a 22-year-old student named Kathy Parks on May 6. In June, two more women were abducted by Bundy, never to be seen again.

Many of his abductions were performed with the aid of a false plaster-cast on his arm. His method was to approach young women and ask them whether they could help him to carry some books or a briefcase.

His most audacious and daring abductions occurred in broad daylight on 14 July in Lake Sammamish State Park in Issaquah, Washington. Five women told police that a man with his left arm in a sling, calling himself 'Ted', had asked whether they could help unload a sailboat from his Volkswagen Beetle. That day two women went missing: 19-year-old Denise Naslund and 23-year-old Janice Ott; the latter was last seen in his company.

> **Five women told police that a man with his left arm in a sling, calling himself 'Ted', had asked whether they could help**

Police circulated the descriptions of 'Ted' and his Beetle throughout the Seattle area, receiving thousands of responses. Among those who reported Bundy as a possible suspect were one of his former psychology professors, his girlfriend and Ann Rule. Their warnings were ignored.

By early September, the remains of Bundy's victims began to turn up around the area of Issaquah. By this point he had already killed two more women and had moved to Utah, where he enrolled at the University of Utah's College of Law.

During that first term, he killed a total of four Utah girls, aged 16 and 17, including the daughter of a police chief. He also saw the escape of one of his intended victims, Carol DaRonch. Bundy lured her into his car on the pretence that he was a police officer. When he attempted to handcuff and beat her with a crowbar she fought back and managed to escape, later providing the authorities with an accurate description of Bundy.

In his second term, beginning in January 1975, he claimed four more victims. The first three, females in their 20s, were each killed in Colorado. The fourth, a 13-year-old named Lynette Culver, Bundy abducted from a school playground in Pocatello, Idaho. He then took her to his room at a nearby Holiday Inn, where she was raped and drowned in the bath. Another young girl, 15-year-old Susan Curtis, was killed during his summer break from law school.

On 16 August 1975, Bundy was arrested when he failed to stop for a police officer. In searching his Beetle police discovered an ice pick, a crowbar, handcuffs and other items that they believed might be burglary tools. Further investigation revealed a more sinister purpose. On 1 March 1976, he was sentenced to 15 years in prison for his kidnapping of Carol DaRonch.

Authorities in Colorado, meanwhile, were pursuing murder charges and by 1977 had enough evidence to charge him with the murder of a woman who had disappeared while on a ski trip with her fiancé. Brought to the Pitkin County courthouse in Aspen on 7 June 1977, Bundy was given permission to visit the

Bundy abducted 12-year-old Kimberly Leach on her way to high school. After raping and murdering her, he hid her body in an abandoned hog shed

courthouse library. From there, he managed to escape by jumping from a second-storey window. He ran, then strolled through the streets of Aspen, making his way to the top of Aspen Mountain. He became lost and disoriented. Six days later, Bundy came upon a car, which he stole. As he drove back to Aspen, two patrol men pulled him over for having dimmed headlights. He was recognized immediately and arrested.

He was imprisoned in a jail in nearby Glenwood Springs, where he was to remain until his murder trial. At some point during the months that followed, he somehow acquired $500 and a hacksaw blade. On the evening of 30 December 1977, ten days before the trial was scheduled to begin, he managed to escape through a crawl space. Seventeen hours passed before Bundy's jailers discovered he'd escaped – though they didn't know it, by that point their famous prisoner had made it all the way to Chicago.

Bundy spent much of the New Year's first week on the road. There is some evidence to suggest that he was considering educational institutions at which he might commit his next assaults. He spent some time at the University of Michigan in Ann Arbor and travelled to Atlanta, before settling in Tallahassee, Florida on 8 January. There, Bundy managed to support himself through shoplifting and purse snatching. On 15 January 1978, two and a half years after his last murder, Bundy killed again. His victims were 20-year-old Lisa Levy and 21-year-old Margaret Bowman, two Florida State University students. At approximately three in the morning, Bundy broke into their sorority house and bludgeoned, strangled, and sexually assaulted the two women. Two other members of the sorority were also beaten. Though severely injured, both survived. Eight blocks away, he invaded another house and beat a fifth student – she, too, survived.

On 9 February, Bundy travelled to Lake City, Florida, where he abducted a 12-year-old named Kimberly Leach from her junior high school. After raping and

Dr Lowell J. Levine, a forensic odontologist, testifies that the bite marks found on the buttock of Lisa Levy show characteristics of Bundy's teeth. Bundy's teeth and the bite marks are displayed behind him

murdering the girl, he hid her body in an abandoned hog shed. Although he returned to Tallahassee, three days later he stole a car and began a journey across the Florida panhandle. Early on the morning of 15 February, he was stopped by a Pensacola police officer and arrested for driving a stolen vehicle. It wasn't long before he was identified and linked to the sorority girl murders.

He received two death sentences – the first for the murders of Lisa Levy and Margaret Bowman, the second for that of Kimberly Leach. During the second trial, Bundy married Carole Ann Boone, a former co-worker, as he was questioning her under oath. A daughter, Tina, was born in October 1982.

Bundy spent much of the 1980s fighting his death sentence. However, as the decade was drawing to a close, it appeared all his legal options had been exhausted. Bundy then began to confess to a number of murders, some unknown to authorities. He promised that more would be revealed if he were given extra time. It was a transparent ploy, and did not work.

On the morning of 24 January 1989, Bundy was executed. He was strapped to an electric chair and for nearly two minutes electricity was sent through his body. His last words were, 'I'd like you to give my love to my family and friends.'

CLIFFORD OLSON

As the media in America focused increasingly on the gruesome acts of psychopaths like Jerry Brudos and Ted Bundy, the situation north of the border seemed markedly different. True, Canada had had its own serial killer – Peter Woodcock, a teenager who had been declared legally insane after murdering three children in the mid-1950s – but his crimes were largely forgotten.

Then, on 17 November 1980, Christine Wheeler, a 12-year-old who lived with her mother and father in a suburban Vancouver motel, went missing. At first, there was no suspicion of foul play; indeed her parents waited several days before filing a missing person's report. Even then, the police treated the case as that of a runaway. It was only after the discovery of her abandoned bicycle behind a nearby animal hospital that the serious nature of the disappearance became apparent. On Christmas Day, her body was discovered in a dump by a man walking his dog. She'd been raped, strangled with a belt, and stabbed multiple times in the chest and abdomen.

Christine Wheeler's murder was the first in a series of savage, sex-related murders that would lay to rest the idea among some Canadians that the serial killer was an American phenomenon.

It was some time, though, before the authorities realized that they were dealing with a serial killer. Indeed, after the Wheeler murder, the murderer lay low for five months. On 16 April 1981, he abducted and murdered a 13-year-old

Clifford Olson was born on New Year's Day, 1940. He was jailed at the age of 14, the first of 83 convictions, ranging from parole violation to armed robbery, before his killing spree began

girl, Colleen Daignault. Five days later, he used hammer blows to the head in murdering his first male victim, 16-year-old Daryn Johnsrude, a Saskatchewan native who was visiting the Vancouver area during his school's Easter break.

As experts then believed that serial killers limited their victims to only one gender, authorities did not initially link the murder of Daryn Johnsrude with those of Christine Wheeler and Colleen Daignault. They did, however, have a suspect in the killings of the two girls: Clifford Olson. In what is certainly the most tragic aspect of the case, the authorities then came upon an even stronger suspect and made him the focus of their investigation. As it turned out, Olson was their man.

The son of a milkman and a cannery worker, Clifford Olson was born in a downtown Vancouver hospital on New Year's Day, 1940. He spent most his youth in the suburb of Richmond. A poor student, it wasn't long before he began skipping classes and committing petty crimes. He was jailed for the first time at the age of 14. Three years later he left school for good, getting a job at a racetrack. It didn't last long. At 17 he was convicted of breaking, entering and theft, and was sentenced to a nearby correctional facility. It would be the first of 83 convictions, ranging from parole violation to armed robbery, before his killing spree began.

Olson's first murder, that of Christine Wheeler, coincided with the news of his live-in girlfriend's pregnancy. The second and third murders occurred during the month in which his only child, Clifford Olson III, was born. The couple married the following month, on May 15 1981, the day after he allegedly assaulted a five-year-old girl, and four days before his fourth murder.

That day, as her boyfriend's mother looked on, Sandra Wolfsteiner was picked up by Olson while hitch-hiking. She was never to be seen again. A month later, a 13-year-old girl vanished after taking the bus to meet a friend. Both mysteries were added to a file that had become known as 'The Case of the Missing Lower Mainland Children'.

It was the disappearance of a sixth child, on 2 July, that propelled the case on to the national stage. At 9 years of age, Simon Partington was unlikely to be a child runaway; this, combined with photographs of his innocent-looking face and descriptions of the Snoopy book he'd had with him when last seen, provoked an emotional public response. The Royal Canadian Mounted Police (RCMP) began what would become the largest manhunt in their history.

The heightened profile of the case had little effect on the killer. In fact, it may well have stimulated his desire to kill. On 9 July, he was driving with a male companion through the city of New Westminster when he spotted 15-year-old Judy Kozma, whom he recognized as a McDonald's cashier. Accepting Olson's offer to drive her to nearby Richmond, where she had a job interview, Kozma joined the pair. Along the way, Olson encouraged the girl to drink, then gave her pills claiming they would help kill the effects of the alcohol. Olson then dropped off his male companion at a suburban shopping mall, and drove out into the country, where he raped and killed Kozma.

Though they hadn't made contact, by this point Olson was once again in the sights of the authorities – and yet the killing continued. Beginning on 23 July Olson murdered a 15-year-old boy, followed by an 18-year-old female German tourist, a 15-year-old girl and a 17-year-old waitress – all within the space of a week.

The end of Olson's killing came when a police surveillance team followed their suspect to Vancouver Island. There they watched as he burgled two Victoria homes, then picked up two young female hitch-hikers. The trio headed into the bush, Olson's driving becoming increasingly erratic. The authorities finally moved in and arrested him for impaired and dangerous driving. In Olson's rented car they discovered an address book belonging to Judy Kozma, which, it was later claimed, he'd used to make threatening phone calls to the dead girl's friends.

Olson was released but remained under surveillance. On 12 August, he was again arrested. Under questioning, he confessed to the murder of Judy

On the day he was arrested, Clifford Olson was trailed by a police surveillance team to Vancouver Island where he proceeded to pick up two young female hitch-hikers, at which point his driving became increasingly erratic

Kozma. Though the RCMP officers were convinced that he was involved in other child murders, they had no idea as to the number; few bodies had been found, and several of Olson's victims were still thought of as runaways.

It was while Olson was under questioning that the case took a controversial turn. He offered to lead police to his victims' bodies, and to provide a detailed account of each murder. In exchange he wanted his wife to be given $10,000–$100,000 per body. 'The first one will be a freebie', he is reported as having said.

The proposal was accepted by the police, Olson did as he'd promised, and the money was delivered. When exposed the following year, the deal was met with public outrage.

21 August 1997: relatives of some of the victims hug after Clifford Olson is denied a hearing with the parole board

Why exactly the RCMP paid Olson can perhaps best be judged by what they had known at the time. The force had a confession for one murder, and suspected Olson of many more. But how many? The high number came as a surprise. Furthermore, only four bodies had been discovered. The money was justified as a small price to pay in order to develop air-tight cases and bring closure to the families of the missing children.

The subsequent trial was swift. After three days Olson was handed down 11 consecutive life sentences.

For his brutal crimes, Olson earned the moniker 'The Beast of BC'. Several books were written, most focusing not on the brutal murders, but on the controversial deal made by the RCMP. Olson served as the inspiration for John Grinell, the serial killer in the 1983 Ian Adams novel *Bad Faith*. Even Olson wrote a book, *Profile of a Serial Killer: The Clifford Olson Story*, in which he refers to himself in the third person. It remains unpublished.

Though Olson took his place in the nation's psyche, he remained out of the news – gone, but not forgotten. However, he was never one to turn down the opportunity to call attention to himself. In 1991, he applied for release under Canada's 'faint hope clause', a section of legislation intended to release those judged truly reformed. The application was turned down. In 2006, having served 25 years of his sentences, he applied for parole, and was again turned down. During the hearing Olson claimed that the three-member panel had no jurisdiction as he'd been granted clemency by the United States government for information he had provided concerning the attacks of 11 September 2001.

Olson was refused parole in 2008 and 2010 and died of cancer in Quebec at the age of 71. As for Peter Woodcock, Canada's first recorded serial killer, on 31 July 1991, after spending 34 years in an Ontario psychiatric facility, he was granted his very first day pass. Within an hour he murdered a fellow psychiatric inmate with a hatchet. Woodcock was apprehended and returned to the facility, where he died on 5 March 2010, his 71st birthday.

GARY RIDGWAY

About 200 kilometres south of the Canadian border, less than a three-hour drive from the area where Clifford Olson had committed his murders, is the mouth of the Green River. A beautiful, if not exactly important river, at one time its main claim to fame would have been as the provider of drinking water for the city of Tacoma, Washington. However, in the summer of 1982, it was used for an entirely different purpose: the disposal of bodies. From that point on, the river mouth, appreciated for its fishing and white water rafting, would be forever linked to Gary Ridgway, a man dubbed 'The Green River Killer'.

Gary Leon Ridgway was born on 18 February 1949 in Salt Lake City, Utah. The middle child in a family of three boys, he was raised in a working-class neighbourhood of Seattle, Washington. His mother ruled the household and is known to have been abusive both mentally and physically to her husband. Ridgway's father drove a city bus near the airport and often complained about the prostitutes who worked along his route.

Ridgway was a poor student and did not finish high school until he was 20 years old. After graduation, he served in the United States Navy. In 1970, while stationed in San Diego, he met and married his first wife. The marriage was a brief one. Shortly after the wedding Ridgway was assigned to a six-month tour of duty, during which his bride took up with another man. Although she accompanied him back to Seattle after he was discharged from the navy, they divorced in 1971.

After a failed attempt to become a policeman, Ridgway found a painting job customizing new trucks in Bellingham, Washington. Both conscientious and meticulous, he found it was work for which he was well-suited. In December 1973 he married for a second time. A son was born within two years. For a time, it seems, Ridgway's second marriage was more stable than had been his first. He developed an intense interest in evangelical Christianity, attempting to save co-workers and neighbours. Though his dedication never ceased, it did dissipate somewhat as his second marriage began to fail. In July 1980, the couple were divorced.

After his second wife left him, Ridgway began frequenting prostitutes, a habit he may have also had in his later teenage years. Within months, he was

The Green River is a beautiful if fairly insignificant stretch of water appreciated for its fishing and whitewater rafting. In the summer of 1982 it became the dumping ground for the bodies of Gary Ridgway's victims

accused of having tried to choke a prostitute on Seattle's airport strip, where his father had once driven the bus. In early 1982, he was stopped by police and questioned after having picked up an 18-year-old named Keli McGinness. In April of that same year, he was arrested after having attempted to solicit an undercover policewoman in a prostitution sting.

That July and August, the bodies of five females, aged between 16 and 31, were found in the Green River. Most of the victims had been prostitutes. The police quickly realized that the deaths were caused by a serial killer. By April 1983, 20 girls and women had vanished. One of the disappeared was a prostitute named Marie Malvar. Her boyfriend had watched as she had got into a dark-coloured truck. He never saw her again. Quite by chance, a few days later, he spotted the truck, followed it to a house on South 348th Street, and called the police. The truck and house belonged to Ridgway. He was questioned briefly by police.

During the late spring and summer of 1983, a dozen more women disappeared, including Keli McGinness, the prostitute who had

Green River killer Gary Ridgway cries in court as he listens to testimony from relatives of his victims. Devoted husband Ridgway avoided the death penalty by agreeing to help police find the bodies of those who were still missing

been with Ridgway when he'd been questioned by police the previous year.

As both the number of disappeared and the body count continued to increase, the Green River Task Force dedicated to catching the killer was inundated with tips and other offers of assistance. Among the interested was Ted Bundy, who from his prison cell contributed in helping to form a profile of the unknown killer. As he'd been raised in Tacoma, Bundy was very familiar with the areas in which the murders were taking place.

One of numerous persons of interest, Ridgway was twice given a polygraph test, in 1984 and 1986, passing both times. After police searched his locker at work and studied his time sheets, co-workers ribbed Ridgway, dubbing him 'Green River Gary'. No one gave any serious thought to the notion that he might be the serial killer.

It was during this period that Ridgway married yet again. By all accounts the marriage appeared to be a happy one. Ridgway was seen as a devoted husband who was said to treat his wife like a queen.

By 1986, it appeared that the Green River Killer had stopped his activities. While bodies were still being found, it was obvious that the victims had been murdered several years earlier. The task force continued, albeit with a lessened staff. In April 1987, they searched Ridgway's home, took a DNA sample, and let him be.

In 1991, nine years after it had begun its work, the Green River Task Force was reduced to a single person. Fifteen million dollars had been spent in its efforts to catch the Green River Killer.

The case remained all but dormant for a decade until, in April 2001, a new sheriff chose to step up the investigation. Among the new initiatives was a DNA analysis of the semen found on the bodies of several of the Green River Killer's victims. Using a new testing method, in September a link was made between the semen's DNA with the DNA obtained from Ridgway in 1987.

Now being watched by the police, on 16 November Ridgway was arrested in another undercover prostitution sting. Three days after appearing in court on the charge, Ridgway was arrested and charged with the murders of Marcia Chapman, Cynthia Hinds, Opal Mills and Carol Ann Christensen, four of the women whose bodies had been found with his DNA.

On 5 November 2003, Ridgway pleaded guilty to the aggravated first-degree murder of 48 women. In doing so, he fulfilled his part of a deal that would spare him the death penalty. Another condition of the agreement was that he would assist in efforts to locate the remains of his victims.

Ridgway claimed that all his victims had been killed in and around the Seattle area. The bodies of two victims had been disposed of 250 kilometres to the south, in Portland, Oregon, in an attempt to confuse the police. Of the women he confessed to murdering 44 were killed between 1982 and 1984, after which he claimed to have committed only four more murders – in 1986, 1987, 1990 and 1998.

Sceptics point out that this bloody history is atypical of serial killers, and speculate that he may have committed murders in other

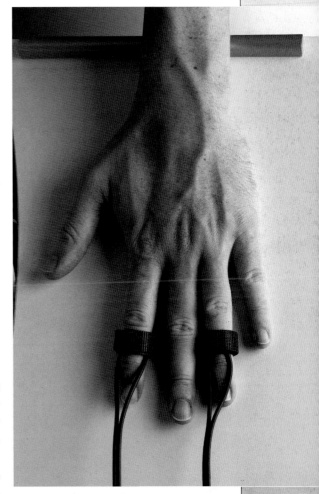

Ridgway twice took polygraph tests, in 1984 and 1986, passing both times

Police Lieutenant Dan Nolan stands beside a display of the Green River Killer's victims, many of whom were left in the forest and picked clean by scavengers. Ridgway may have killed many more women than he was arraigned for

locations. Some point to a series of 40 prostitutes murdered in and around San Diego from 1985 to 1991. During those years, it is thought that Ridgway travelled to the city as his son was then living there. Other theories put forth the idea that he was involved in the disappearance of some of the approximately 60 women who vanished from the streets of Vancouver's Downtown Eastside from the early 1980s through to 2002.

On 18 December 2003, Ridgway received 48 life sentences with no possibility of parole and an additional life sentence to be served consecutively. He is currently incarcerated at Washington State Penitentiary in Walla Walla, probably still claiming that the murders were committed for the betterment of society.

AILEEN WUORNOS

Dubbed 'the first female serial killer' by a lazy media, during the closing years of the 20th century and the beginning of the 21st, Aileen Wuornos was a media star.

Wuornos had an unenviable beginning. She was born Aileen Carol Pittman in Rochester, Michigan, on that rarest of days, 29 February, in 1956. Wuornos' parents had married when her mother was just 15 years old. Less than two years into the marriage, her father, Leo Dale Pittman, left his wife Diane, who was pregnant with Aileen. This abandonment was a blessing in disguise, as he would later be convicted as a child molester. Diagnosed as a paranoid schizophrenic, he spent much of his remaining years in mental hospitals. In 1969, Pittman hanged himself in his prison cell, never having met his daughter.

When she was four years old, Wuornos and an older brother, her only sibling, were abandoned by their mother. The children were legally adopted and raised by their Finnish grandparents in Troy, Michigan. Wuornos claimed that until the age of 12 she had thought them to be her true parents. She also maintained that as a child she had been sexually abused by her grandfather and had suffered beatings at the hands of both grandparents.

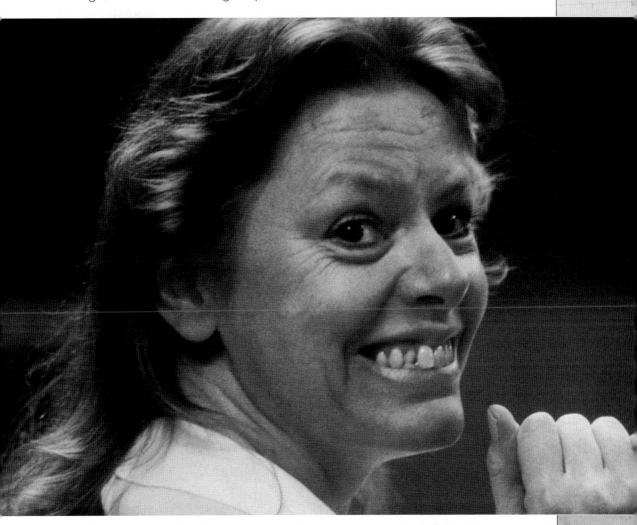

Aileen Wuornos had a disturbing upbringing. At the age of four, she was abandoned by her mother and brought up by grandparents. She says she was abused by her grandfather and suffered regular beatings

Though she was sexually promiscuous from an early age, Wuornos' claim that her brother counted among her many partners is suspect. In 1970, at the age of 14, she became pregnant. The child, a baby boy born on 23 March 1971, was adopted and never knew his birth mother. Four months later, her grandmother died of liver failure, a condition exacerbated perhaps by the unwanted pregnancy. Diane Wuornos accused her father of having killed her mother. The children were made wards of court.

> While still in high school, Aileen turned to prostitution... She soon began to have trouble with the law

While still in high school, Aileen turned to prostitution, at first offering sexual favours in return for food, drink and cigarettes. She soon began to have trouble with the law stemming from incidents related to drinking. At the age of 18, Wuornos was first jailed in Jefferson County, Colorado, charged with drunk driving, disorderly conduct and firing a gun from a moving vehicle. A further charge of failing to appear in court was added after she returned to Michigan.

The year in which Wuornos entered her 20s, 1976, would prove to be highly eventful. That spring, her grandfather committed suicide through gas inhalation. On 13 July, she was charged with assault after throwing a cue ball at a bartender's head. Four days later, Wuornos' brother died of throat cancer, leaving her as the beneficiary of his life insurance. She received $10,000 and spent the money within two months. One of her purchases was a luxury car, which she subsequently wrecked.

That September, Wuornos hitch-hiked to Florida, where she was picked up by a wealthy retired man named Lewis Fell. Though he was 49 years her senior, the two were married before the end of the year. The event was covered on the society page of the local newspaper. Fell bought his new bride a car and jewellery.

The marriage was neither peaceful nor enduring. Wuornos continued her drinking and fighting in local bars and was soon jailed for assault. As it entered its second month, Fell had the marriage annulled.

She turned increasingly to crime as a means of support. In 1981, Wuornos held up a supermarket in Edgewater, Florida, while dressed in a bikini. She was quickly apprehended and charged with armed robbery. As a result, she spent most of 1982 and 1983 in prison. In 1984, she was again incarcerated after having attempted to pass forged cheques at a bank in Key West. In 1986 alone, Wuornos was accused of speeding, grand theft auto, resisting arrest, obstruction and having attempted to rob a male companion at gunpoint.

That summer, while drinking in a Daytona gay bar, she met a 24-year-old motel maid named Ty Moore. The two became lovers later that same evening, and were soon living together. Wuornos encouraged Moore to quit her job and allow her to support them both through her earnings as a prostitute. Although the romantic and sexual elements of their relationship soon ended, they remained together in a transient lifestyle that took them through Florida. Wuornos took to travelling with a concealed pistol, which she made a point of keeping loaded.

By 1989, she was finding it increasingly difficult to support herself and Moore through prostitution. Now 33, she was finding that her market value was diminishing; years of drinking and drug abuse were taking their toll.

That December, Wuornos committed her first known murder. The victim was Richard Mallory, the 51-year-old owner of a Clearwater electronics repair shop. Though a secretive man, he was known to have gone off on bouts involving drinking and sex. He picked up Wuornos and drove into the woods outside Daytona Beach. Once there, they shared a bottle of vodka, after which Wuornos shot him four times, and stole the contents of his wallet. Wuornos then went home and told Moore what she had done.

While hitch-hiking in May 1990, she was picked up by a 43-year-old heavy equipment operator named David Spears. Wuornos shot Spears six times, then stole his truck, which she later abandoned.

On 6 June, she flagged down her next victim, 40-year-old Charles Carskaddon. Wuornos shot him six times, stole his gun, his money and his jewellery, and drove off in his car. The next day she dumped the vehicle and began hitch-hiking. Wuornos was soon picked up by Peter Siems, a 65-year-old retired merchant seaman who was on his way to visit relatives in Arkansas. A man devoted to his work in Christian outreach, he was travelling with a stack of Bibles. Wuornos murdered Siems and stole his car. This time she chose to keep her

Richard Mallory was Wuornos' first victim – she told the court that she acted in self-defence after he had raped her

victim's vehicle, a reckless decision that would lead eventually to her capture.

On 4 July, while driving with Moore outside Orange Springs, she wrecked Siems' car. Though no other vehicles were involved, the pair made a great scene, swearing and pleading with a witness not to call the police. They attempted to continue their journey, but soon had to abandon the vehicle. After the car was found to belong to Siems, who had long been reported missing, accurate descriptions of Wuornos and Moore were sent out nationwide.

Wuornos killed three more men, the last on 19 November 1990. Just days later, newspapers across Florida ran a story about the killings, along with sketches of the two women seen walking away from Siems' stolen car. Wuornos and Moore were quickly identified. Sensing that the authorities were closing in, Moore left Wuornos while she was out buying alcohol.

On 6 January 1991, Wuornos was arrested and charged with an old weapons violation. Moore was tracked down to her sister's home in Pittston, Pennsylvania. She would later assist police, allowing them to tape jailhouse phone conversations between herself and Wuornos, which were used at trial. Fearing that Moore would be implicated in the murders, on 16 January Wuornos confessed, adding that her killings had been in self-defence as all her victims either had raped or had intended to rape her.

> Wuornos was executed by lethal injection. In her final interview, she said she expected to be taken away by angels in a spaceship

It wasn't until the following January that Wuornos was first put on trial. In the intervening year, she had attracted a great deal of media attention, and had even sold the screen rights to her life story. It was a tale she told many times and in many versions. The murders were also covered by numerous inconsistent stories. Then, too, there were the wild claims, one being that as a prostitute she had had sex with 250,000 men. In order to have reached this number she would need to have had sex with an average of 35 different men each and every day beginning at the age of 15 – and yet, this and other improbable statements were passed on by various media outlets without comment.

On 27 January 1992, she was found guilty of Mallory's murder. At the verdict, she shouted to the jury, 'I'm innocent! I was raped! I hope you get raped! Scumbags of America!' The trial that followed would hear several similar courtroom outbursts. In all she was found guilty of six murders. Although she had confessed to murdering Siems, along with the others, she was not charged, as no body was ever found.

On 9 October 2002, Wuornos was executed by lethal injection at Florida State Prison. She became the tenth woman to be put to death in the United States since the reintroduction of the death penalty in 1976. In her final interview, Wuornos said that she expected to be taken away by angels in a spaceship

ANDREI CHIKATILO

Even as the USSR retreats into history, there is something almost surreal in the grouping of the words 'Soviet serial killer'. Rightly or wrongly, the phenomenon often seems so much a symptom of the West. How incredible, then, that a serial killer from the Soviet Union was more prolific and, one might claim, more sadistic than any of his western contemporaries. Andrei Chikatilo is thought to have raped and killed at least 52 people of both sexes. He mutilated their bodies, often in ways reminiscent of Jack the Ripper.

Andrei Romanovich Chikatilo was born on 16 October 1936 in Yablochnoye, a village in what is now the Ukraine. As a child he suffered terribly, growing up with the after-effects of the Ukrainian famine. His mother often told him a story that he'd had an older brother, Stepan, who had been kidnapped and then consumed by starving neighbours. No documentary evidence supports the existence of this sibling.

After the Soviet Union entered the Second World War, when he was four, his father went off to fight. Chikatilo was left alone with his mother, sharing her bed each night. A chronic bed-wetter, he was beaten for each offence. As the war progressed, he was witness to the Nazi occupation and the massive devastation and death caused by German bombing raids. Dead bodies, not an uncommon sight, were things he found both frightening and exciting.

The end of the war brought little happiness to the Chikatilo household. His father, who had spent much of the conflict as a prisoner of war, was transferred to a Russian prison camp.

Awkward and overly-sensitive, Chikatilo withdrew from other children. He was considered a good student, but failed his entrance exam to Moscow State University. In 1960, after finishing his compulsory military service, he found work as a telephone engineer It was during this period that Chikatilo,

The Ukrainian famine of 1932-33: Chikatilo's mother told him an older brother, Stepan, had been consumed by starving neighbours

now 23 years old, attempted his first relationship with a woman. He found himself unable to perform sexually, a humiliation that his prospective girlfriend spread among his acquaintances. As a result, he developed elaborate fantasies of revenge in which he would capture the woman and tear her apart.

When Chikatilo married, in 1963, it was through the work of his younger sister, who made the arrangement with one of her friends. He suffered from chronic impotence, yet managed to father a son and daughter. Late in life it was discovered that he had suffered brain damage at birth, which affected his ability to control his bladder and seminal emissions.

In 1971, after completing a degree in Russian literature through a correspondence course, he managed to get a teaching position at a local school. Though a poor instructor, Chikatilo continued in the profession for nearly a decade, often dodging accusations that he had molested his students.

In 1978, having accepted a new teaching position, Chikatilo moved to Shakhty. Living alone, waiting until his family could join him, he began to fantasize about naked children. Chikatilo bought a hut off a shabby side street from which he would spy on children as they played, all the while indulging in his solitary practices. Three days before Christmas, he managed to lure a nine-year-old girl, Yelena Zabotnova, into his lair. He had intended to rape the girl, but found himself unable to achieve an erection. He then grabbed a knife and began stabbing the girl, ejaculating in the process. He later disposed of the girl's body by dumping it into the Grushovka River. Chikatilo was a suspect in the crime; several witnesses had seen him with the girl and blood was discovered on his

Police photos of Chikatilo with the black bag which contained the knives used on his victims: because the Soviet Union controlled the media, reports of rape and serial murder were suppressed, greatly aiding perpetrators

doorstep. However, another man, Alexsandr Kravchenko, confessed to the murder under torture. Kravchenko was subsequently executed.

Chikatilo's good luck did not transfer to his new school. In 1981, he was dismissed after molesting boys in the school dormitory. Through his membership of the Communist party, he was soon given a position as a supply clerk at a nearby factory.

Though he did not kill again until the 3 September 1981 murder of Larisa Tkachenko, Chikatilo had begun a series of murders that lasted until the month of his capture, 12 years later.

Chikatilo most often preyed on runaways and prostitutes who, like Fritz Haarmann before him, Chikatilo found at railway and bus stations. Enticing his victims with the promise of cigarettes, alcohol, videos or money, he would lead them into nearby forests. The corpse of one young female runaway, discovered in 1981, is typical of the horrific scenes Chikatilo would leave behind. Covered by a newspaper, she was lacking her sexual organs. One breast was left bloody by a missing nipple. Chikatilo later admitted that he had bitten and swallowed it, an act which caused him to ejaculate involuntarily.

His male victims, all of whom ranged in age from 8 to 16, were treated in a different manner. It was Chikatilo's fantasy that each was being held as prisoner for some undisclosed crime. He would torture them, all the while fantasizing that he was a hero for doing so. Chikatilo would offer no explanation as to why, more often than not, he would remove the penis and tongues while his victims were still alive. Many of his early victims had their eyes cut out, an act performed in the belief that they would provide a snapshot of his face. The practice all but stopped when, upon investigation, Chikatilo realized this to be an old wives' tale.

There can be little doubt that Chikatilo was aided in his crimes by the state-controlled media of his time. Reports of crimes like rape and serial murder were uncommon, and

The body of Tanya Petrosan, 32, who was murdered in 1984: Chikatilo enticed victims with the promise of cigarettes, alcohol, videos and cash

In a world where censorship ruled, rumours got out of hand: many believed a werewolf was the killer

seemed invariably to be associated with what was portrayed as the hedonistic West. While close to 600 detectives and police officers worked on the case, staking out bus and train stations, and interrogating suspects, those living in the areas where the bodies were found were entirely unaware that there might be a serial killer in their midst. Still, with over half a million people having been investigated, there were bound to be rumours. One story had it that boys and girls were being mauled by a werewolf. It was not until August 1984, after Chikatilo had committed his 30th murder, that the first news story was printed in the local party daily.

On 14 September 1984, there was a break in the case when an undercover officer spotted Chikatilo approaching various young women at the Rostov bus station. When questioned, Chikatilo explained that, as a former schoolteacher, he missed speaking with young people. The explanation did nothing to allay suspicions and the officer continued to trail Chikatilo. Eventually, the former teacher approached a prostitute and, after having received oral sex, was picked up by the police. His briefcase, when searched, was found to contain a kitchen knife, a towel, a rope and a jar of petroleum jelly.

So certain were the authorities that they had their serial killer that the prosecutor was asked to come and interrogate Chikatilo. However, any celebration was cut short when it was discovered that Chikatilo's blood type did not match that of the semen found on the victims' bodies. This discrepancy, which has never been satisfactorily explained, is most often considered the result of a clerical error. After two days, Chikatilo was released, having admitted to nothing more than soliciting a prostitute.

There is the possibility that Chikatilo would have remained under interrogation for a longer period had it not been for the fact that he was a member of the Communist party. This association would quickly come to an end weeks after his near-capture when he was arrested and charged with petty theft from his workplace. Chikatilo was expelled by the party and sentenced to three months in prison.

After his release, Chikatilo found new work in Novocherkassk. His killing began again in August 1985 and remained irregular for several years. By 1988, however, he seemed to have returned to his old ways, murdering at least nine people. And yet it appears he took no life during the calendar year that followed. In 1990, he killed nine more people, the last being on 6 November, when he mutilated Sveta Korostik in the woods near the Leskhoz train station.

Andrei Chikatilo's behaviour in court was peculiar and disruptive, veering from exaggerated yawning to singing and talking gibberish. Twice he dropped his trousers and exposed himelf to those surrounding his iron cage

With the station under surveillance, Chikatilo was stopped and questioned as he emerged from the area where the body would later be discovered.

On 14 November, the day after Sveta Korostik's body was discovered, Chikatilo was arrested and interrogated. Within the next 15 days, he confessed to and described 56 murders. The number shocked the police, who had counted just 36 killings during their investigation.

Chikatilo finally went to trial on 14 April 1992. Manacled, he was placed in a large iron cage in the middle of the courtroom. It had been constructed specially for the trial, primarily to protect him from the families of his victims. As the trial got underway, the mood of the accused alternated between boredom and outrage. On two occasions Chikatilo exposed himself, shouting out that he was not a homosexual.

Chikatilo's testimony was equally erratic. He denied having committed several murders to which he'd already confessed, while admitting his guilt in others which were unknown. Claiming other murders as his own seemed less bizarre than other statements. At various points Chikatilo announced that he was pregnant, that he was lactating and that he was being radiated. On the day the prosecutor was to give his closing argument, Chikatilo broke into song and had to be removed from the courtroom. When he was returned and offered a final opportunity to speak, he remained mute.

On 14 October 1992, six months after his trial had begun, Chikatilo was found guilty of murdering 21 males and 31 females. All of the males and 14 of the females had been under the age of 18.

Throughout the trial Chikatilo's lawyer had made repeated attempts to prove that his client was insane, but a panel of court-appointed psychiatrists dismissed the claim. An appeal having been rejected, on St Valentine's Day, 1994, Chikatilo was taken to a special soundproof room and executed with a single gunshot behind his right ear.

JACK UNTERWEGER

Jack Unterweger entered prison as an uneducated murderer and emerged a celebrated author. The toast of Vienna, he was feted and invited to openings and soirées – but his real interest was in murdering prostitutes.

He was born Johann Unterweger on 16 August 1950 to a prostitute in Judenburg, Austria. He never knew his father, nor did he know the man's identity. However, it was generally assumed then, as now, that Unterweger's father was an American soldier. Abandoned at birth, for his first seven years he was raised in extreme poverty by an alcoholic grandfather in a one-room cabin.

From an early age Unterweger displayed a wild and unpredictable temper. At 16, he was arrested for the first time after having assaulted a woman. Tellingly,

Unterweger's victim was a prostitute. Other crimes followed in quick succession; he was charged with stealing cars, burglary and receiving stolen property. He was also accused of having forced a woman into prostitution and taking all the proceeds.

On 11 December 1974, he and a prostitute named Barbara Scholz robbed the home of an 18-year-old German prostitute named Margaret Schäfer. Afterwards, Schäfer was taken by car into the woods, where Unterweger tied and beat her. Then he removed her clothes and demanded sex. When she refused, he hit her with a steel pipe and she was strangled with her own bra. He was quickly caught. In his subsequent confession, Unterweger tried to defend his actions by saying that it was his mother whom he'd envisaged beating, and not Margaret Schäfer.

Unterweger was sentenced to life in prison for the murder. Having received little in the way of schooling as a child – he entered incarceration as an illiterate – he found prison could provide him with an education. His progress was dramatic. He soon learned to read and write, and developed an interest in the literary arts. In a short time, he was writing poetry, plays and short stories, as well as editing the prison's literary magazine.

> Unterweger tied and beat her. Then he removed her clothes and demanded sex. When she refused, he hit her with a steel pipe and strangled her

In 1984, his first book, an autobiography entitled *Fegefeuer – eine Reise ins Zuchthaus* ('Purgatory: A Journey to the Penitentiary'), was published to great acclaim and went on to become a bestseller. Unterweger was soon giving interviews and publishing essays and more books – very much the public person, despite being incarcerated. In 1988, his life story – or part of it, at least – was played out on the silver screen when *Fegefeuer* was made into a feature film. Unterweger became a *cause célèbre* among those promoting the ideals holding prison as a place in which criminals can be reformed.

On 23 May 1990, having served 15 years of his life sentence, Unterweger was granted parole. Thus, he began a new life involving opening nights, book launches and exclusive receptions. Articulate, handsome and stylish, Unterweger was in demand as both a talk show guest and a dinner guest. His career as a writer seemed to go from one height to another; he was sought-after as a journalist his plays were being performed throughout Austria.

Before long, as a journalist, he was covering a beat he knew well: murder.

Because prostitution is legal in Austria, it was felt that 'women of the streets' were better protected than they really were. Investigators were slow to realize the epidemic of murders was the work of one man

Much of his writing concerned a number of prostitutes who had recently been murdered. He put both his past and celebrity to good use, moving freely through the streets. In his writing and in television pieces he berated the authorities for not having solved the crimes, asserting that there was a serial killer in Austria who was preying on prostitutes.

The first of these prostitutes, Brunhilde Masser, had last been seen alive on 26 October 1990 on the streets of Graz. Less than six weeks later, another prostitute, Heidemarie Hannerer, disappeared from Bregenz, near the border with Germany and Switzerland. Her body was discovered on New Year's Eve by two hikers. Upon inspection, it was apparent that she had been strangled with a pair of tights. Though she was fully clothed, it was after her death that she had been dressed. On 5 January 1991, Masser's body was found outside Ganz. Though badly decomposed, the corpse revealed that she too had been strangled with tights.

On 7 March, another Austrian prostitute, Elfriede Schrempf, disappeared. By this point the authorities were becoming extremely concerned. Since it is a legal occupation in Austria, prostitution has fewer dangers than in many other western nations. In an average year,

> **Heidemarie Hannerer's body was discovered on New Year's Eve. Upon inspection, it was apparent that she had been strangled with tights**

the country would suffer no more than one murdered prostitute. And yet, in little more than four months two prostitutes had been murdered and another had gone missing. Worries increased when Schrempf's family received two phone calls in which they were threatened by an anonymous man. Though unlisted, their number was one that Schrempf carried on her person.

On 5 October, hikers discovered Schrempf's remains in the woods outside Graz. Within a month, another four prostitutes would disappear from the streets of Vienna. Looking at all the evidence, a team of investigators from Ganz, Bregenze and Vienna concluded that the murders and disappearances were not the work of a serial killer, a finding with which Unterweger took issue.

Another person who disagreed with the team's findings was August Schenner. A 70-year-old former investigator, Schenner had been involved in solving the 1974 murder of Margaret Schäfer, for which Unterweger had served his prison time. He noted that Schäfer had been strangled, as had another prostitute whom he had always suspected Unterweger of killing. And, of course, all the recent murders of prostitutes had been committed by means of strangulation. When the bodies of two of the missing prostitutes surfaced, both strangled, the authorities became convinced that they did indeed have a serial killer on their hands – and that he was most likely Jack Unterweger.

> **Police discovered Unterweger had been in Graz on the dates when Brunhilde Masser and Elfriede Schrempf had disappeared**

The celebrity author was placed under surveillance for three days. On the fourth day, Unterweger flew off to Los Angeles, where he was to write an article on crime in the city for an Austrian magazine. In his absence, the Austrian federal police tracked their suspect's movements since his release from prison. They discovered that he had been in Graz on the dates when Brunhilde Masser and Elfriede Schrempf had disappeared; in Bregenze when Heidemarie Hannerer had been murdered, and in Vienna when all four prostitutes had gone missing. They also learned that Unterweger had visited Prague in September 1990. A call to Czech authorities revealed that they had an unsolved murder of a young woman, Blanka Bockova, dating from that time. When found by the bank of the Vitava River, her body had a pair of grey stockings knotted around the neck.

After he returned from Los Angeles, Unterweger was questioned by officers of the criminal investigation bureau. One of the officers already knew the suspect as he'd been interviewed by the celebrity author for one of the articles he'd written on the murders. Unterweger denied knowing any of the prostitutes, saying that his knowledge of their respective fates was limited to what he'd found through his work as a journalist. He was let go due to lack of evidence. Soon thereafter, he resumed his attacks in print for what he described as the mishandling of the case.

In their hunt for evidence, the police discovered that Unterweger had sold the car he'd first bought after his release from prison. With the permission of the new owner, they went through the vehicle and discovered a hair fragment which, through DNA testing, was shown to be that of Blanka Bockova. With the hair sample, investigators now had enough to obtain a search warrant for Unterweger's apartment.

A call to the Los Angeles Police Department brought news that three prostitutes had been strangled during Unterweger's time in the city.

When Austrian police moved in to arrest Unterweger, they discovered that he had left the city, ostensibly to holiday with Bianca Mrak, his 18-year-old girlfriend. In reality, he was fleeing to avoid arrest. Unterweger managed to enter the United States by lying about his previous murder conviction. He settled with Mrak in Miami, from where he launched a campaign against the Austrian authorities. At the centre of his fight was the accusation that the police were fabricating evidence in an attempt to frame him. Connections in the media were called upon in an effort to have his version of events published.

On 27 February 1992, Unterweger was arrested by United States marshals after he picked up money that had been wired to him. They arrested him on the grounds that, in lying about his 1974 murder conviction, he had entered the country illegally. He fought deportation until he learned that California, the state in which he was suspected of murdering three prostitutes, had the death penalty.

Special knowledge: Unterweger occupied a strange position where as a 'resocialized' ex-con and best-selling author he was in a position to duplicitously comment in the media on crimes he had actually committed

On 28 May, he was returned to Austria. There Unterweger was subject to a law which permitted him to be charged for the murders he was accused of committing both inside and outside of the country's borders – 11 in total. Awaiting trial, Unterweger gave interviews and wrote letters to the media in which he professed his innocence. He was convinced that the public was on his side. However, the tide had long since begun to turn; even his former friends in the media doubted his innocence. Unterweger went on trial in June 1994 with the conviction that his popularity and charm would win over the jury.

On 29 June 1994, Unterweger was found guilty of all but two charges of murder. He was sentenced to life in prison without parole. That evening Unterweger used the string of his prison jumpsuit to hang himself. The knot he tied was the very same one he'd used on his victims.

JEFFREY DAHMER

In the very early morning of 27 May 1991, a naked boy was spotted staggering on a city street in Milwaukee, Wisconsin. His body bore signs of trauma and he appeared to be in a confused state. Paramedics arrived on the scene, followed closely by three members of the Milwaukee Police Department. They were met by a tall blond man who identified himself as Jeffrey Dahmer. The naked boy, Dahmer claimed, was his 19-year-old lover. He explained the boy's incoherence by saying that they had been drinking, adding that his 'lover' had wandered off while he was out buying more beer.

The officers accompanied Dahmer and the boy back to the apartment. There they found photographs of the boy in his underwear. The teenager was made to sit on the couch, next to his folded clothing. Against the boy's objections, he was left in the care of Dahmer. The police then left the apartment – a flat later described as well-kept and neat, though it did have an unpleasant odour.

The boy they left behind wasn't 19, as Dahmer had claimed, but a 14-year-

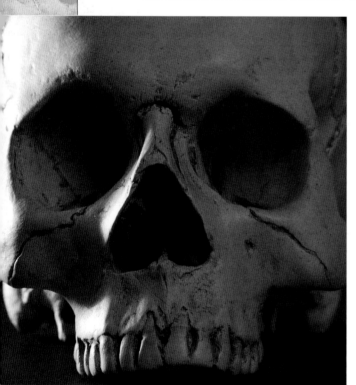

Jeffrey Dahmer had a fixation with the skulls of his victims, which he often kept as souvenirs

old named Konerak Sinthasomphone. He was anything but Dahmer's lover. In the hours following Sinthasomphone's return, courtesy of the Milwaukee police, Dahmer strangled and dismembered the boy, but not before having sex with his corpse. His skull was kept as a souvenir. Dahmer would later provide an explanation for the boy's confused state by revealing that he had drilled a hole in the teenager's skull.

Four more young men would share similar fates, all at the hands of the tall blond man who, within two months, would become one of the most infamous serial killers in American history.

Dahmer was born in Milwaukee on 21 May 1960. Very much a wanted child, he began life as a happy, if slightly sickly, boy. His personality dampened somewhat at the age of 6 after he underwent an operation for a double hernia. That same year, the family relocated to Ohio, a move which troubled Dahmer. He developed a dislike of the new and unfamiliar, while at the same time becoming increasingly withdrawn and uncommunicative.

Lionel and Shari Dahmer stand outside the Columbia Correctional Institute which housed Jeffrey

He was incapable of maintaining friendships, and preferred to be alone. Much of his time, it was later discovered, was spent on a secret animal cemetery he had created from roadkill found when cycling around the community. The centrepiece was a dog's head he had mounted on a stake. The dedication and hard work Dahmer put into his cemetery was absent from other areas of his life. An intelligent teenager, lacking in motivation, he achieved nothing more than average grades, and began to drink.

When he was 18 years old, his parents divorced. Following years of tension and acrimony, the decision could not have come as a surprise. There followed a bitter custody battle over his only sibling, a younger brother named David.

Dahmer committed his first murder in June 1978, the same month in which he'd graduated from high school. The victim was a 19-year-old named Steven Hicks, a hitch-hiker whom Dahmer had spotted while driving. The two returned to the Dahmer home, where they drank beer and had sex.

When Hicks expressed his wish to leave, Dahmer, unable to bear the thought of being left alone, killed the hitch-hiker by striking him with a barbell. He then cut up the body, placed it in rubbish bags, and buried it in the woods behind his house, adjacent to his pet cemetery. Years later he would dig up

Hicks' corpse, pound it with a sledgehammer and scatter the remains.

His father soon remarried and, with his new wife, encouraged Dahmer to enrol in Ohio State University. He spent his only term there drinking. His father then laid down the law, telling his eldest son that he could either get a job or join the army. Continuing to drink, making no attempt to seek employment, in January 1979 Dahmer was driven to a recruiting office. He was enlisted to serve a six-year stint in the United States Army. Interestingly, he appeared to take to life in the military – at least initially. But after two years he was discharged, owing to his excessive drinking.

After a few months in Florida, he returned to his family in Ohio. Arrested for drunkenness and disorderly conduct, in 1982 he was sent off to live with his grandmother in Wisconsin. His troubles with the law only escalated. In August,

Dahmer was charged with public exposure after drunkenly dropping his pants at the Wisconsin State Fair. Four years later, in September 1986, he was arrested for masturbating before two boys and was put on probation for one year.

The following September he committed his second known murder, killing 26-year-old Steven Toumi, with whom he had been drinking in a gay bar. Using a large suitcase, Dahmer managed to move Toumi's body from the scene of the crime, a hotel room, to his grandmother's basement. There he used the corpse for a variety of sex acts, before dismembering and disposing of it in the trash.

The next month he killed Jamie Doxtator, a 14-year-old boy who was seen frequently outside various gay nightclubs. In March 1988, he struck again, murdering Richard Guerrero, a 25-year-old who Dahmer claimed he met in a gay bar.

On 25 September 1988, Dahmer moved out of his grandmother's house

A mugshot from 1982, when Dahmer was arrested for indecent exposure at the Wisconsin State Fair

and into an apartment in Milwaukee. The very next day, he offered a 13-year-old boy $50 to pose for some photographs. The boy went to Dahmer's new home, where he was drugged and fondled. The crime was discovered after the teenager's parents, concerned as to his state, took him to the hospital where it was confirmed that their son had been drugged. Dahmer was arrested while at his job, working as a mixer for the Ambrosia Chocolate Company.

GRISLY SOUVENIR

Dahmer returned to his grandmother's house to await trial. In February, he met a 24-year-old aspiring model, Anthony Sears, and brought him back to the house to pose for photographs. Instead, Dahmer drugged and strangled Sears. He then had sex with the corpse, dismembered it, and placed the head in boiling water. Once he had managed to remove the skull, he painted it so that those who might see his souvenir would think it was plastic.

For Dahmer's assault on the 13-year-old boy, he was sentenced to one year of 'work release', under which he was permitted to work during the day so long as he returned to prison each evening. Though he pleaded guilty, Dahmer claimed in his defence that he had thought the boy was much older than 13.

In an awful coincidence, Dahmer's victim was the brother of Konerak Sinthasomphone, whom he would murder less than two years later.

Dahmer served ten months of his sentence before being let out early for good behaviour. A letter from Dahmer's father, urging that his son not be released until he had received treatment, was ignored. He was registered as a sex offender and began what was intended to be a five-year term of probation.

After a couple of months in his grandmother's house, on 14 May 1990, Dahmer moved into his own flat in a complex called the Oxford Apartments. The following month he committed his sixth murder. He killed again in July and twice in September. There was then a five-month gap. His first murder of 1991 wasn't committed until February. A 19-year-old named Errol Lindsey was killed in April, before Dahmer began the spree that would lead to his capture. May saw two more victims, the second being Konerak Sinthasomphone.

Then, on 30 June 1991, beginning with the killing of a man named Matt Turner, Dahmer began a string of murders averaging one every five days: Jeremiah Weinberger on 5 July, Oliver Lacy on 12 July, and Joseph Bradeholt on 19 July.

He experimented with various methods in disposing of the bodies, using a variety of acids and chemicals. The resulting sludge Dahmer poured down the drain or flushed down the toilet. He ate the flesh of selected victims and would often keep one or two body parts, usually the skull and genitals.

Neighbours began to complain about the vile smells coming from Dahmer's apartment. When confronted, he offered a variety of explanations, including spoiled meat and a dirty aquarium. The sounds of sawing were also heard. It

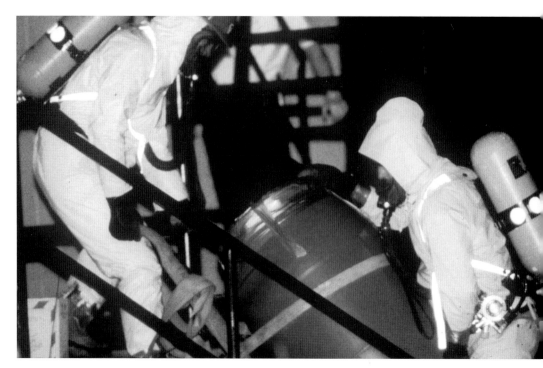

Policemen take away dismembered body parts from Dahmer's apartment. Officers were criticized for the way the case was conducted, but no one was asked to pay for mistakes which cost victims their lives

was observed that stray cats swarmed whenever he threw anything into the dustbin. Yet, it wasn't the complaints of his fellow residents that brought the killing to an end; it was Dahmer's next intended victim.

On 22 July 1991, police spotted a short, athletic man named Tracy Edwards running with handcuffs dangling from one wrist. Assuming he'd somehow escaped police custody, they confronted him and were told that he had escaped a man who had threatened his life. He led the police back to Dahmer's apartment. The horror of Dahmer's secret life was finally exposed.

GUILTY AND SANE

Eventually charged with 15 counts of murder, Dahmer's trial began the next summer. Such was the nature of his crimes that the authorities felt it unnecessary to charge him with the attempted murder of Tracy Edwards. Initially, Dahmer pleaded not guilty by reason of insanity; then, against the wishes of his lawyer, he changed the plea to guilty, while maintaining his claim of insanity. In the end, the jury found him to be both guilty and sane. He was sentenced to 15 life terms; a total of 937 years in prison. In a statement made before the court Dahmer expressed remorse for the killings, adding that he wished for his own death.

Dahmer's wish came true on 28 November 1994, when he and a fellow

inmate were beaten

After the horrors
John Balcerzak and
Konerak Sinthasomp
Had they bothered to
have learned he was
Had they bothered to
have discovered the b
Dahmer's bed. An au
after the incident, lau
public. A witness to the
left a message for the
a local newspaper. The

In 1991, Balcerzak
Department. On appeal
was elected president o

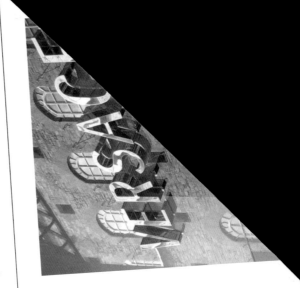

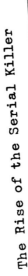

ANDREW

Had they not been mur Lipper, Mary Ann Nichols, Annie Chapman, Elizabeth Stride, Catherine Eddowes and Mary Kelly would be names forgotten by history. These women were, after all, just five among thousands of prostitutes who worked the streets of Victorian London. During their lives they were not people of note; they became so after their deaths. The fame attained by victims of multiple murderers comes through the actions of their killer.

In this respect, the name Gianni Versace stands apart from the others. An accomplished clothing and costume designer, he was one of the most important and talented figures in the fashion world of the late 20th century. In 1995, his label had a profit of $900,000,000. On the morning of 15 July 1997, returning from his customary stroll along Ocean Drive in Miami, Florida, he was shot twice in the head outside his oceanfront mansion. He was the fifth and final victim of 27-year-old serial killer Andrew Cunanan.

Born on 31 August 1969 in San Diego, California and raised in the nearby community of Bonita, Cunanan appeared blessed. The baby of the family, he and his brother and sisters lived in comfort, seeming to want for little. Although it was true that his parents' marriage was a troubled one, Cunanan appeared able to ignore the tension, retreating to his room where he would immerse himself in the escapist plots of comic books and adventure novels.

When Andrew was a child, his father, a Filipino-born officer in the United States Navy, retired from service and remade himself as a stockbroker. His youngest son left the public school system and was enrolled in the prestigious Bishop's School.

Highly intelligent, Cunanan excelled at his new school. It was said that he displayed fluency in seven languages. He was attractive and well-liked. The openness which he displayed concerning his homosexuality appeared not to dampen his popularity among the student body.

As early as 15, he was frequenting the more popular gay bars in San Diego. In order to hide his age and ethnicity, Cunanan began to adopt different personas. As Andrew DaSilva or David Morales, he would change manner of dress from one evening to the next, often fooling those with whom he had been socializing the previous evening. When he graduated from Bishop's School in

Versace is a 'high-end' international fashion house with clients like Elton John, Michael Jackson and Jennifer Lopez

1987, Cunanan was listed as 'most likely to be remembered'.

At his parents' urging, Cunanan enrolled as a history student at the University of California, but his bar-hopping had a detrimental effect on his work. Though 18, he was already a three-year veteran of San Diego's gay bar scene. During that period, he had come to recognize that his good looks, youth, polish and taste had a certain value among the more mature homosexual patrons. Cunanan sought and obtained the attention and generosity of older men. As an 'associate' or 'secretary', he accompanied successful lawyers, property developers, executives and other wealthy gay men to society functions. From one of these men, he received a $30,000 car; others gave him credit cards.

As Cunanan's wealth increased, his parents were feeling the financial strain. The former naval officer hadn't been much of a success as a stockbroker and had been fired by several agencies. The last dismissal brought with it a charge that he had embezzled $106,000. Deserting his wife, Cunanan's father fled the country. She was forced to sell the family home and move into a more modest house in a less desirable area. It was at about this time that she discovered her youngest son was gay. When confronted, Cunanan pushed his mother with such force that she suffered a dislocated shoulder.

After quitting university, Cunanan visited his father, now living in the

Philippines. He was ashamed to find the man who had once taken such pride in his appearance reduced to living in a shack. Partly to earn money for his return to the United States, Cunanan soon gravitated to the local gay scene.

SPLIT PERSONALITY?

He ended up in San Francisco, where he again began to adopt new personalities, the most popular being Drew Cummings, a gay navy lieutenant. Among the new group of older gay men the city offered was a well-connected lawyer named Eli Gould. Soon Cunanan found himself at parties attended by supermodels and celebrities. It was at one of these events that he was approached by Versace. The story goes that the designer mistook Cunanan for someone else – and that the young San Diegan, so used to pretending to be someone he wasn't, never bothered to clarify things.

However, there was a side of Cunanan beginning to emerge that was anything but glamorous. He began to act in pornographic films featuring sadistic sexual acts. He took pleasure in humiliation and pain. Acquaintances couldn't help but notice his darkening moods. Though he was still welcome at the parties of the beautiful people, he had begun to misbehave. He made the rounds at one event describing *Friends* actress Lisa Kudrow as a 'bitch', after she'd left without saying goodbye. After failing to earn a walk-on part in a Hugh Grant film, he accused the actor of having personally blocked hiring him. The peculiar behaviour was reflected in his bedroom, which he had converted into a shrine dedicated to Tom Cruise. He openly expressed his jealousy for the actor's then wife Nicole Kidman.

By 1997, the wealthy older homosexual men had moved on. Cunanan was now 27. As Cunanan's youth faded away, so too did his health. He began to display symptoms associated with AIDS and convinced himself that he had the disease. Early in the year, he underwent tests, but never returned for the diagnosis. Had he

Andrew Cunanan ended up in San Francisco and soon showed he wasn't about to play the shrinking violet

done so, Cunanan would have learned that the results were negative. He began to gain weight and his once neatly groomed hair became long and unkempt. His sharp mind was dulled by vodka and painkillers, in which he would also deal as a means of support.

In April, the brooding, jealousy, drinking and drug abuse apparently came

Gianni Versace, seen on the catwalk in Paris in 1996, was one of the most important figures in fashion. Tragically, at the height of his fame, he became the fifth and final victim of serial killer Andrew Cunanan

together with fatal results. Cunanan had become convinced that two of his lovers, architect David Madson and Jeffrey Traill, a former naval officer, were seeing each other behind his back. Though they had not known each other at the time, both had lived in California when they first met Cunanan. In the intervening years, they'd relocated to Minneapolis, where they were finally introduced to one another by their mutual friend.

On the receiving end of an angry phone call from Cunanan, Traill denied that he was seeing the architect. On 26 April, Cunanan flew to the Minneapolis-St Paul airport, where he was picked up by Madson. According to friends, the plan was to sit down and allay Cunanan's suspicions. The meeting, scheduled for the following day, did not go as planned. Cunanan became enraged, grabbed a hammer from a kitchen drawer and bashed in Traill's skull.

> **The meeting did not go as planned. Cunanan became enraged, grabbed a hammer from the kitchen drawer and bashed in Traill's skull.**

Cunanan and Madson rolled the corpse of the former naval officer in a Persian rug. During the next two days the pair attempted to behave as if nothing unusual had happened. Their cover was blown when the building manager of Madson's loft complex came upon the body. Cunanan and Madson learned of the discovery and fled Minneapolis in the architect's Jeep Cherokee. Seventy kilometres out of town, they pulled over to the verge on a country lane, and Cunanan put three bullets into Madson's head. The gun, which he had brought with him from San Francisco, had once belonged to his friend Traill.

On 4 May, in Chicago, he tortured and killed a highly successful 72-year-old developer named Lee Miglin. After making himself a meal, Cunanan spent the night in the Miglin home. The next morning, he left in the developer's 1994 Lexus, but not before he drove repeatedly over his corpse, reducing it to mush.

Cunanan made no attempt to hide his identity – indeed, it appears he was taunting the authorities. When discovered in the vicinity of Miglin's home, Madson's Jeep Cherokee had his pictures covering the front seat. Cunanan was placed on the FBI's Top Ten Most Wanted list.

ON THE RUN

On 9 May, seeking to dump the Lexus, he shot and killed William Reese, a 45-year-old caretaker at Finn's Point National Cemetery in Pennsville, New Jersey. Before long, driving Reese's stolen truck, he arrived in Miami Beach, Florida. He checked into the rundown Normandy Plaza Hotel, where he rented a room by the month.

Murder weapon: the Taurus semi-automatic .40 S&W calibre which Cunanan used to kill Gianni Versace and two other victims before turning it on himself

During the two months leading up to Versace's murder, Cunanan would frequent the city's gay bars and clubs. It is thought that many of his days involved walks around the neighbourhood where the designer's mansion was. On 15 July, the morning on which he committed his final murder, he had followed Versace home from a local café.

With the designer's murder, Andrew Cunanan became a household name, but the heightened awareness appeared to provide no boost to the ongoing manhunt.

In the end, despite the hue and cry that had erupted throughout the city, it was not the FBI or the Miami Beach Police Department that found Cunanan, but a Portuguese caretaker who, checking on a client's houseboat, startled the killer. A standoff ensued, ending with the police entering the houseboat and finding Cunanan dead on the floor. He had committed suicide using Traill's gun – the same weapon with which he'd murdered three of his five victims.

It can be said that a tragedy of errors contributed to the death of Gianni

Versace. The Miami Beach Police Department had received confirmed sightings of Cunanan, but had failed to make this information public. Thus, the murderer was able to move freely and without suspicion within the city's gay community.

Though abandoned, Reese's stolen truck sat for over two months before it came to the attention of the police.

Eight days before Versace's murder, Cunanan had boldly used his own identification and the Normandy Plaza Hotel address in pawning some gold coins he had stolen from the Miglin home. The information was then faxed to the Miami Beach Police Department, as required by law. There it was placed on the desk of a clerk who was away on holiday. It was discovered a few hours after Versace's murder.

The most incredible of all these many mistakes came when a SWAT team invaded and searched a Normandy Plaza room in which Cunanan was supposed to have been staying. Not only did they not find the murderer, it appeared neither traces nor clues had been left behind. Two days later, hotel staff realized they had given the authorities the incorrect room number.

Versace's house on South Beach where he was shot twice by Cunanan – once point blank in the face and the other in the neck. The 50-year-old designer died instantly, but lay on the steps for 20 minutes before the ambulance came

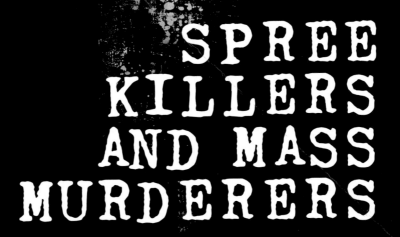

SPREE KILLERS AND MASS MURDERERS

The earliest and most extreme recorded acts of mass murder are those committed by groups, including armies and states. As with serial killings, most acts of mass murder by individuals have taken place in recent decades. Shootings at schools and workplaces have increased dramatically and a new term was added to the lexicon: the 'spree killer', one who embarks on a murderous rampage, claiming victims in more than one location.

GEORGE HENNARD

George Hennard considered Steely Dan's 'Don't Take Me Alive' to be his theme song. The lyrics of this very bleak piece of music, inspired by the constant eruptions of violence in 1970s Los Angeles, concern a cornered murderer who is surrounded by police. Whether he knew it or not – and it is likely that he did – Hennard would one day be in a very similar position.

George Hennard was born on 15 October 1956, the son of an army surgeon and his wife. He had a difficult relationship with his mother, and would depict her in drawings with a serpent's body. After graduating from high school in 1974, he joined the United States Navy, and later the Merchant Marine. In 1989, after 15 years of service, Hennard was dismissed for possessing a small amount of marijuana. The end of his duty left him extremely depressed. He told a judge, 'It means a way of life. It means my livelihood. It means all I've got. It's all I know.' Although he underwent drug treatment, he became increasingly reclusive.

He lived alone in a large, two-storey colonial-style house in Belton, Texas, the seat of Bell County. Belonging to his mother, this once grand home had fallen into disrepair, a state that had led to several confrontations with local officials. A good-looking man, Hennard appeared to have a great deal of problems with women. Those who knew him best often described him as a misogynist. He was given to shouting obscene remarks at women as they passed his home, and appeared threatening to his neighbours.

In the winter of 1991, while on a trip to Nevada, he bought a 9mm Glock-17 semi-automatic pistol and a 9mm Ruger. In May, Hennard was carrying one of the guns when he was arrested by a park ranger in Lake Mead, Nevada, for driving while intoxicated and carrying a loaded weapon.

The next month, Hennard expressed his bitterness towards women in a five-page letter to Jill Fritz and Jana Jernigan, two sisters who lived down the street. Made public within 24 hours of the shooting, it is a rambling, venomous document. Hennard begins by mistakenly referring to the young women as 'Stacee' and 'Robin'. It reads, in part, 'Do you think the three of us can get together some day? Please give me the satisfaction of someday laughing in the face of all those mostly white treacherous female vipers from those two towns who tried to destroy me and my family.' At another point in the letter, Hennard expresses

> Hennard had a difficult relationship with his mother, and would depict her in drawings with a serpent's body

his appreciation of the sisters: 'It is very ironic about Belton, Texas. I found the best and worst in women there. You and your sister are the one side. Then the abundance of evil women that make up the worst on the othe side.' Hennard included photographs of himself and concluded by asking that the two women not disclose the contents of the letter to anyone other than their immediate family.

Although Hennard considered Jernigan and her sister to be on the opposite side of 'the abundance of evil women', she was not spared his threatening phone calls. The sisters' mother was also on the receiving end of his abuse. Both approached police with their concerns, fearing that he would one day explode into violence.

Though disconcerting, none of these communications would have been particularly newsworthy, had it not been for a ten-minute incident which took place on 16 October 1991, the day after Hennard's 35th birthday. That day, he

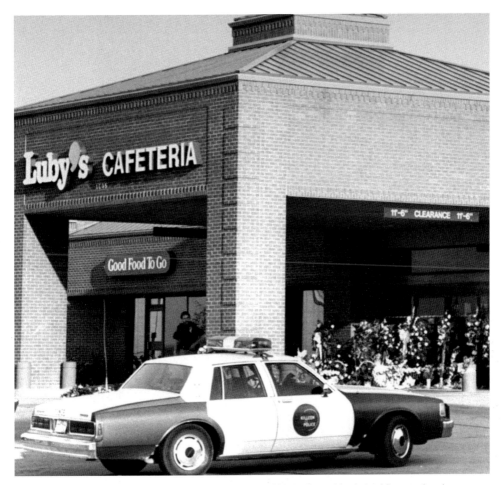

A police car stands guard outside Luby's Cafeteria complete with wreaths and baskets of flowers placed there by mourners for those killed in the massacre by psychopathic gunman George Hennard

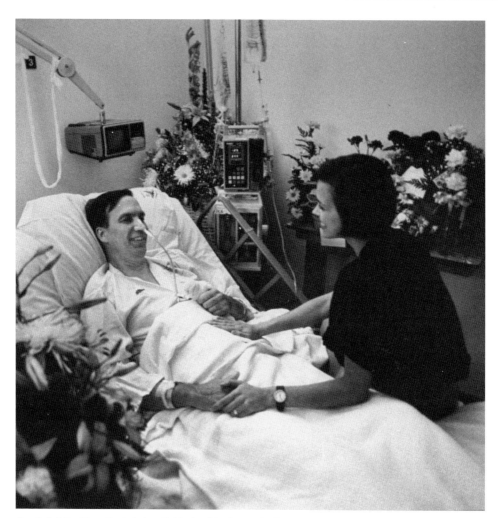

Gunshot victim Steve Ernst chats with his daughter Amy as he lies in hospital convalescing from wounds to the stomach. He was one of the lucky ones: 23 people died in the worst mass shooting in the history of Texas

left his Belton home and drove 25 kilometres to Killeen, the largest city in Bell County. At about 40 minutes after noon, he drove his blue Ford Ranger pick-up into the parking lot of Luby's Cafeteria, a chain restaurant situated on the interstate highway. Hennard gunned the engine and rammed the truck through the restaurant's plate glass window, striking an elderly male diner. The assumption was that there had been a terrible accident, and several members of the lunchtime crowd rushed to help. He then emerged from the cab with his Glock and Ruger.

'This is what Bell County has done to me!' he yelled, and began to shoot.

The first person to die was the man he had struck with his pick-up; Hennard shot him in the head. He was methodical in his killing, making certain that each was dead or mortally wounded before moving on to the next victim.

At one point he paused and spoke to a woman with a 4-year-old girl, saying 'Get the baby and get out of here, lady, right now.' He then returned to firing, shooting the woman's mother. Witnesses later said that he appeared to focus on shooting women.

There were some patrons who managed to escape. One man hurled himself through one of the restaurant's plate glass windows, creating an opening through which others followed. Those who could not escape sought to hide themselves behind overturned tables.

Police arrived at the bloody scene ten minutes into the slaughter. They exchanged fire and hit the gunman four times. Hennard sought refuge in one of the restaurant washrooms, where he committed suicide by shooting himself in the head.

It was then the worst mass shooting in the history of the United States: 14 women and nine men lay dead; one other victim was mortally wounded. Another 20 people had been injured, some by glass as they'd tried to escape through the broken window.

The first paramedics to enter later reported discovering people playing dead, despite the fact that the shooting had ceased minutes earlier. One Luby's employee had to be treated for hypothermia after spending over two hours hiding in the restaurant freezer, unaware that the gunman was dead. Another hid for nearly 24 hours in a commercial dishwasher before being discovered.

After the shooting, Luby's Cafeteria was closed for five months. It never regained the popularity it had once enjoyed. In 2000, the restaurant shut its doors for good.

Two days after the shooting, a proposed ban on semi-automatic assault weapons that had been before the United States Congress failed. However, the Texas shootings did have a lasting legacy; one that was markedly different than that of the Montreal Massacre, which had taken place less than two years earlier. As students at the Ecole Polytechnique pushed for tighter gun control laws north of the border, a survivor of the Killeen shooting was crossing the United States campaigning in support of concealed handgun laws. Suzanna Hupp had been eating at Luby's when Hennard began his shooting spree. Although she managed to escape, both her parents, who had been at the table with her, were killed without mercy.

She had left her handgun in her truck as Texas state law then forbade the carrying of a concealed weapon. Hupp argued that she would have had an opportunity to stop the killing if she'd been permitted to carry the handgun in her handbag. Today she is credited with having helped to bring about the state's current concealed weapons law.

In 1998, she became the first woman to be awarded a lifetime membership of the National Rifle Association.

THOMAS HAMILTON

Though 43, Thomas Hamilton had never had any adult friends. He preferred to spend his time with young boys. He displayed all the signs of paedophilia, yet no reliable evidence has ever been produced that he sexually abused anyone.

Hamilton was born Thomas Watt on 10 May 1952 in Glasgow. Shortly thereafter, his parents separated and in 1955 were divorced. Just before his fourth birthday, he was adopted by his maternal grandparents, who changed his name to Thomas Watt Hamilton. He grew up believing that his birth mother was his sister. It wasn't until 1985, when Hamilton was in his 30s, that the woman he thought was his sister finally moved out of the parental home. Two years later, Hamilton and his adoptive parents moved into the house in which he would live for the rest of his life. By the end of 1992, Hamilton's adoptive mother had died, while his adoptive father had moved into an old people's home. At the age of 40, he was for the first time living away apart from his adoptive parents.

Hamilton had participated in boy scouts as a child, an interest that continued into adulthood. In 1973, he was appointed assistant scout leader to a troop in Stirling. Although he had passed the various checks made into his suitability, it wasn't long before complaints were being made about his leadership. The most serious of these concerned two occasions when boys were forced to sleep in a van overnight in his company. Confronted with the first complaint, Hamilton explained that the intended accommodation had been double-booked. When the situation repeated itself, an investigation was undertaken which revealed that there had been no booking on either occasion. As a result, he was removed from his position and, ultimately, his name was added to a blacklist.

All the signs were there that Thomas Hamilton was a serious potential danger to children, yet nothing was ever done about it

In the years that followed, he made several attempts to return to scouting. In February 1977, Hamilton requested that a committee of inquiry be formed to address a complaint that he had been victimized. The request was denied. The following year, he failed in an attempt to bypass the blacklist by offering his services in another district.

Frustrated in his attempts to again participate in scouting,

Hamilton became increasingly involved in boys' clubs. Beginning in the late 1970s, Hamilton organized and operated at least 15 different clubs, three of which, the Dunblane Boys' Club, the Falkirk Boys' Club and the Bishopbriggs Boys' Club, he was active in at the time of his death.

Hamilton's clubs were aimed primarily at boys between the ages of 8 and 11. For the most part, activities consisted of gymnastics and games. Although he was on occasion assisted by others, including parents, more often than not Hamilton ran each club entirely on his own. He employed a title, 'The Boys' Clubs Sports Group Committee', in order to create the impression that other adults were involved in the running of the clubs. In reality, there was no such body.

When he became unemployed in 1985, the fees provided Hamilton with a small source of income. In most cases, the clubs began as extremely popular operations – some attracting approximately 70 boys – but would invariably start to decline. His ideas of discipline tended not to match those of the boys' parents. The fitness regimes were strenuous and harsh, leading volunteers and parents to consider them militaristic. Some went so far as to suggest that Hamilton was taking pleasure in dominating the boys.

> **Hamilton received complaints regarding his insistence that boys wore tight black swimming trunks during gymnastics**

It was noted that Hamilton showed an unusual interest in certain boys, appearing to have favourites. He received complaints from some parents regarding his insistence that the boys wore tight black swimming trunks during gymnastics. Once these were provided by Hamilton, the boys were obliged to change in the gymnasium, rather than the changing rooms.

Also disconcerting was his habit of taking photographs of the boys as they posed in their trunks. In 1989, he added video to his collection of images. When confronted by parents, Hamilton would explain that the photographs and videos were taken for training and advertising purposes. Those parents who saw the videos couldn't help but notice that the boys looked unhappy and uncomfortable. What's more, Hamilton's camerawork appeared to linger on certain parts of the boys' bodies. Hamilton's home contained hundreds of photographs of boys – many wearing black swimming trunks – hanging on the walls or in albums.

Whenever a boy was pulled out of one of his clubs, Hamilton would respond by writing the parents long letters in which he would complain of the rumour and innuendo associated with his activities. He would often hand-deliver these intimidating letters at night.

There were some parents, however, who supported Hamilton. When, in 1983, his leases at two high schools were cancelled when former issues with the scouts came to light, Hamilton obtained 30 letters of support from parents. The lease was subsequently reinstated.

In addition to the boys' clubs, Hamilton would run summer camps. These usually catered for boys of about 9 years of age who might be 12 or so in number. Exactly how many camps Hamilton ran is unknown. His claim that the July 1988 summer camp on Inchmoan Island on Loch Lomond was his 55th cannot be confirmed. Nevertheless, it was the first to be visited by the authorities. Acting on a complaint, two police officers inspected the camp on 20 July, to find the boys ill nourished and inadequately dressed. As one of the constables was involved in scouting, Hamilton dismissed their findings as part of a conspiracy launched by the Scouts' Association. After another of his summer camps, held in July 1991, was investigated, Hamilton replaced the programme with what he termed a 'residential sports training course', in which boys slept on the dining room floor of Dunblane High School. This, too, was investigated by the authorities.

> **Two police officers inspected the camp to find the boys ill nourished and inadequately dressed. Hamilton dismissed their findings**

By 1995, the rumour and innuendo that Hamilton had complained about in letters to parents was putting an end to his clubs. Three had had to shut down due to declining enrolment, while a proposed new club was cancelled when only one boy attended. On 18 August, he circulated letters in Dunblane intended to counter what he described as false and misleading gossip which had been circulated by scout officials. He sought to break free from his reputation by opening up a new boys' club some 40 kilometres away in Bishopbriggs.

Complaints against Hamilton were now being made on a frequent basis. However, while his conduct was of great concern, it had not yet crossed the line into criminality.

At shortly after eight on the morning of 13 March 1996, a neighbour saw Hamilton scraping ice off a white rental van outside his Stirling home. They shared what the neighbour would describe as a normal conversation. Some time later Hamilton drove the van 10 kilometres north to the town of Dunblane, arriving at about 9:30 at the car park of Dunblane Primary School. Parking

A photograph taken by Dunblane schoolteacher Gwen Mayor shows children from her Primary One class just weeks before Hamilton entered the school gym and killed Mayor together with 16 of her pupils

beside a telegraph pole, he cut the wires. It is supposed that Hamilton thought they served the school, when in fact they were for adjoining houses. Beneath his jacket he wore four holsters which held two 9mm Browning semi-automatic pistols and two .357 Smith and Wesson revolvers. He was also wearing a woollen hat and ear protectors. Picking up a large camera bag, Hamilton walked across the car park and entered the school by a side door.

It was a little more than half an hour into the school day when Hamilton entered the gymnasium. There he found two teachers, an assistant and a class of 28 pupils, ranging between 5 and 6 years of age. Hamilton walked forward a few steps, raised his pistol and began firing rapidly and indiscriminately. He hit the physical education teacher, Eileen Harrild, four times, including a shot to the left breast. The other teacher, 47-year-old Gwen Mayor, was killed instantly. The assistant, Mary Blake, was also shot, but managed to seek refuge with several children in a storage area, out of the line of direct fire.

Hamilton remained in his position and continued to shoot, killing one child and injuring others. Still firing indiscriminately, he began to advance further into the gymnasium. He then walked over to a group of the injured and fired at point-blank range.

Although he resumed the wholesale firing, some of Hamilton's shots were more directed. He fired at one boy who was passing by the gymnasium, but missed. Another shot was taken through a window, and was probably directed

Michael Howard was Home Secretary at the time of the massacre, after which the public called for tighter gun controls and restrictions on handguns

at an adult who was walking across the playground. Again, he missed.

He walked out of the gymnasium and fired four shots towards the school library, hitting a staff member, Grace Tweddle, in the head. He then sprayed the outside of a classroom hut, but hit no one.

The teacher, Catherine Gordon, had instructed her pupils to get down on the floor just moments before the shots entered the classroom.

Hamilton re-entered the gymnasium, again shooting haphazardly. He then dropped the pistol and drew a revolver. Placing the muzzle in his mouth, he pulled the trigger.

It is estimated that Hamilton's rampage lasted between three and four minutes and the damage that he caused during that time was absolutely appalling. On the floor of the gymnasium 15 children and their teacher, Gwen Mayor, lay dead. Hamilton had shot these 16 people 58 times. One more child, Mhairi Isabel MacBeath, would die on the way to hospital; 13 other people had received gunshots. All were taken to Stirling Royal Infirmary.

As great as the carnage was, it could have been much, much worse. It wasn't until 9:41, approximately one minute after Hamilton had killed himself, that police received an emergency call.

The first officers arrived on the scene at 9:50. Hamilton was shown to have entered the school with 743 rounds of ammunition, of which he used 106. He used only one of the two 9mm Browning semi-automatic pistols. Both .357 Smith and Wesson revolvers remained in their holsters until Hamilton used one to commit suicide.

ERIC HARRIS AND DYLAN KLEBOLD

Together Eric Harris and Dylan Klebold had many dreams. They wrote of elaborate plans for a major explosion on a par with the Oklahoma City bombing. Another scheme involved hijacking a plane at Denver International Airport, flying 2,600 kilometres, and crashing into a building in New York. Ultimately, they chose as their target a public building they knew better than any other: their own high school. Had everything gone according to plan, their rampage, known as the Columbine High School Massacre, would have been the worst school shooting in history.

Eric David Harris was born on 9 April 1981 in Wichita, Kansas, the second son of a part-time caterer and a United States Air Force transport pilot. In July 1993, the family relocated to Littleton, Colorado. They lived in rented accommodation for three years, eventually buying a house in an upper middle-class neighbourhood close to Columbine High School.

Dylan Bennet Klebold, a native of Colorado, was born in Lakewood on 11 September 1981, 20 years to the day before the events of 9/11. His mother was an employment counsellor and his father had a small, home-based real estate business.

Harris and Klebold met as boys while attending middle school. They had much in common. In 1996, Harris set up a website devoted to Doom, a violent computer game in which players must kill demons and zombies to reach higher levels of play. Also posted on the site were jokes and brief entries concerning

Eric Harris was cited as 'a very bright individual likely to succeed in life' after an anger management course

Dylan Klebold attended his high school prom with a date only three days before the shooting spree

his parents, friends and school. It wasn't long before Harris began to add instructions on how to make explosives, and records of the trouble he and Klebold were causing. The site had few visitors and attracted little attention until late 1997 when the parents of Harris' former friend, Brooks Brown, discovered that it contained death threats aimed against their son. Further investigation by the sheriff's office revealed other threats directed at the students and teachers of Columbine High School, where Harris and Klebold were students. Harris had posted remarks concerning his hatred of society and the desire he had to kill.

A few months into the investigation of the website, in January 1998, Harris and Klebold were caught in the act of stealing computer equipment from a van. They attended a joint court hearing, where it was decided that they both needed psychiatric help. The pair avoided prosecution by participating in a programme that involved three months of counselling and community service. Although both expressed regret publicly, in his journal Harris wrote of his cleverness in deceiving the judge.

Image released by the Jefferson County sheriff office after the massacre

Not long after the court hearing, Harris removed the section of his website in which he'd posted his thoughts and threats. However, as the date of the massacre drew near, he added a new section in which he kept a record of his gun collection and bomb-making activities. Also included was a 'hit list' of those he wished to target. The sheriff's office wrote a draft affidavit for a search warrant of the Harris house, but this was never filed.

Exactly when Harris and Klebold began planning their massacre has been a matter of some debate. However, what can be said with certainty is that their actions were not the result of a whim. Over the course of several months, Harris and Klebold had built their bombs and gathered their ammunition. Well aware that they would be made famous by their actions, Harris left behind a collection of videos in which the two discuss their motivations. Harris recalled that as a member of a military family he had had to move from town to town, always having to start afresh. He also expressed resentment of his brother Byron, who was extremely popular and an accomplished athlete. Parents excepted, Klebold spoke about the grievances he had with his family, who he felt always treated him as their inferior.

The pair relished the place they would stake in history through their actions. Hollywood, they were certain, would fight over the rights to their story. The two discussed who might make the better film – Steven Spielberg or Quentin Tarantino?

They were so dedicated to the documentation of their designs that they made a tape just prior to their departure for the high school. Klebold, the first to speak, announces, 'It's a half-hour before our Judgement Day.' After saying goodbye to his parents, he adds, 'I don't like life very much... Just know I'm going to a much better place than here.'

Harris' farewell is much more rushed. 'I know my mom and dad will be in shock and disbelief,' he says. 'I can't help it.'

'It's what we had to do,' Klebold adds. They spend some time creating something of a video will, listing various belongings that they want to go to friends. When Klebold determines that it is time to go, Harris concludes, ' That's it. Sorry. Goodbye.'

What followed did not go according to plan. Everything had been mapped in such great detail, and yet the events that took place on that sunny Tuesday in April were largely the result of improvisation.

Harris and Klebold planned the massacre to begin in the late morning of 20 April 1999. Their first step was planting a firebomb in a field not far from the school. Set to explode just prior to the start of their assault on the school, it is assumed to have been placed as a diversion for emergency personnel.

They made a tape prior to their departure. Klebold, the first to speak, announces, 'It's a half hour before our Judgement Day.'

The bomb did detonate, though only partially. The small fire it caused was easily extinguished by the local fire department.

The pair arrived at the school in separate cars and parked in different parking areas. Klebold walked over to where Harris had parked. There they armed two 9 kg propane bombs, enough to destroy the cafeteria and bring down the library above as well. With five minutes to detonation, they carried duffel bags containing the bombs into the cafeteria, left them on the floor, and returned to their respective cars. En route to his car, Harris encountered Brooks Brown, and warned him: 'Brooks, I like you. Now get out of here. Go home.'

Harris and Klebold's plan was to wait and fire upon students fleeing the explosion. However, when both bombs failed to detonate, Klebold went back to Harris' car. Carrying duffel bags containing a 9 mm semi-automatic rifle, a 9 mm semi-automatic pistol, two sawn-off 12-gauge shotguns and a number of explosive devices, they walked together towards the cafeteria entrance, and stopped on the outdoor steps.

At 11:19, the pair pulled out their shotguns and began firing at the students.

A security camera catches Harris and Klebold working out why their bombs didn't detonate before they started shooting. Harris once wrote, 'If you disagree I would shoot you... some people go through life begging to be shot.'

Their first shots were directed at two students eating lunch on the lawn. One of the two, a girl, became the first fatality. Although Klebold entered the cafeteria briefly, presumably to determine why the bombs had not detonated, the pair focused for the first minutes on the outside of the high school. While shooting, they began to throw pipe bombs on the lawn, the roof and into the car park. Like the cafeteria bombs, these all proved to be duds.

Five minutes after the first shot was fired, a sheriff's deputy who happened to be at the campus began exchanging fire with the gunmen. While this was happening Dave Sanders, a teacher, managed to evacuate the cafeteria through a staircase leading up to the second floor.

Harris and Klebold ran into the school and proceeded down two corridors, shooting and throwing pipe bombs. They eventually entered the library, where they shot out the windows and began to fire at the police officers outside. The gunmen then turned around and set their sights on students who had been hiding under tables. In the next 7 minutes, Harris and Klebold killed 10 people and injured 12 others.

When the gunmen left the library, they proceeded to the science area, firing indiscriminately. Coming across locked classroom doors, they would peer inside at the students, but make no attempt to gain entry.

The gunmen returned to the cafeteria, where Harris attempted without success to detonate one of the failed propane bombs. The gunmen drank from cups students had left behind on the tables and looked out of the windows, watching as emergency vehicles arrived. They then left and wandered around the school's main corridors. Again, they looked at students through the windows of locked classroom

> After setting a Molotov cocktail alight, Klebold watched as Harris killed himself; seconds later he took his own life

doors, but never attempted to enter the rooms. They paused outside a washroom entrance, taunting the students inside by saying that they were about to enter and kill whomever they found. However, the pair did not go in; rather they continued to wander, seemingly without aim.

At 12:05, nearly half an hour after they'd left, Harris and Klebold re-entered the library to find it nearly empty. All but two survivors had managed to get away – one pretended to be dead and the other, Patrick Ireland, was unconscious. The gunmen attempted to shoot at police officers through the windows, without success. After setting a Molotov cocktail alight, Klebold watched as Harris killed himself; seconds later he took his own life.

Two and a half hours later, Ireland regained consciousness. He crawled out through the window, where he was picked up by SWAT team members. It would be nearly another hour before the police officers finally entered the library. By this time, Harris and Klebold had been dead for just under three and a half hours. It was estimated that nearly 800 police officers circled the school that day – but not one of them entered the building while the two gunmen were still alive.

Harris and Klebold's shooting spree lasted approximately 49 minutes; all those killed or injured were shot during the first 16 minutes. Witnesses report that after they'd killed their final victim both gunmen remarked that the thrill had gone out of shooting people.

JEFF WEISE

Although he committed suicide at the early age of 16, Jeff Weise left behind more writing than any other spree killer in history. His numerous contributions to websites like nazi.org provide glimpses into a truly troubled mind. Six months before committing mass murder, Weise posted on the internet an animated short film he had created. Lasting just 30 seconds, the work features a gunman who kills four people and blows up a police car. The animation ends with the gunman taking his own life. In posting the clip, Weise used the alias 'Regret'.

Jeffrey James Weise began his short unhappy life on 8 August 1988, the son of Daryl Lussier Jr and Joanne Weise. He lived most of his first ten years with his mother in a mobile home outside a Minneapolis pickle factory. On occasion, he would be sent five hours north to see his father on the Red Lake Indian Reservation. These visits ended when his father committed suicide following a day-long stand-off with members of the Red Lake Police Department. One of the officers on the scene was Weise's grandfather, Daryl Lussier Sr, who despite his best efforts was unable to save his son. Jeff Weise was 8 years old. Even before the death of his father, the boy was at the mercy of Joanne Weise, a physically abusive alcoholic. In 1999, she sustained brain damage in an automobile accident, and was confined to a Minneapolis nursing home.

Jeff Weise, who had attempted suicide, was an admirer of Adolf Hitler

Weise, an Ojibwa, was sent to live with his grandfather on the reservation, 390 kilometres away from his former home. He expressed a great deal of frustration in attempting to adapt to his new surroundings. His troubles continued after he entered Red Lake High School, located on the reservation. Eventually, he was pulled out of the school and put on a home schooling programme.

On one of his internet profiles, Weise wrote that he was being given anti-depressants and was seeing a therapist. In fact, he had been prescribed Prozac after twice trying to kill himself. The first attempt took place in the spring of 2004. He later posted an account of the incident on the internet: 'I had went through a lot of things in my life that had driven me to a darker path than most choose to take. I split the flesh on my wrist with a box opener, painting the floor of my bedroom with blood I shouldn't have spilt. After sitting there for what seemed like hours (which apparently was only minutes), I had the revelation that this was not the path.'

With the use of a belt pulled taut around his neck, Weise made his second failed attempt a few months later.

Increasingly, Weise found a forum for expression through the internet. He participated in a number of websites by posting messages and Flash animations. At a site devoted to zombie fiction, he contributed a number of short stories. Weise also visited chatrooms and discussion groups. Under the usernames NativeNazi and todesengel (German for 'angel of death'), he posted frequently on the website of the Libertarian National Socialist Green Party, an organization incorporating elements of Nazi ideology, libertarianism and the environmental movement.

Weise wrote of his admiration for Adolf Hitler and expressed despair over what he saw as interracial mixing among Native Americans. He wrote that he had been unjustly suspected of planning to shoot people at his old high school on 20 April 2004, the 115th anniversary of Hitler's birth. The idea, he added, was that of someone else. In fact, on 19 April, Red Lake High School had received an anonymous warning that a drive-by shooting would take place the next day. The fifth anniversary of the massacre at Columbine High School also happened to fall on the same day.

On the morning of 21 March 2005, as part of his home schooling programme, Weise was visited for an hour by his teacher, and later by a relative. In the mid-afternoon he shot and killed his grandfather while the 58-year-old

A couple embrace at the site of a memorial near the Red Lake High School to the people gunned down by Weise. The killings began after he shot his sleeping grandfather and then rapidly spiralled out of control

man was sleeping. When Lussier's girlfriend, a fellow police officer named Michelle Sigana, arrived at the house, she too was killed.

Weise took his grandfather's police-issue 12-gauge shotgun, 9mm Glock 17, utility belt and bullet-proof vest. He then drove his grandfather's marked patrol vehicle the five-minute-long route to Red Lake High School.

Shortly before three o'clock Weise, now wearing his grandfather's bullet-proof vest, walked through the school's main entrance. He was confronted by Derrick Brun, an unarmed security guard who was manning the school's metal detectors. Weise killed Brun and then turned his guns on a teacher and students, firing as he walked down the corridor. When they fled into a classroom, the gunman followed, killing the teacher and several students. Weise returned to the corridor, running and shooting at random. He attempted to enter a classroom, but a quick-thinking teacher had locked the door.

Less than 10 minutes after the shooting began, four members of the Red Lake Police Department arrived at the school. On entering, they became targets for Weise. In the exchange of gunfire, Weise was hit in the hip and leg. He retreated to a classroom where he took his own life with a shotgun blast to the head.

Weise's rampage at the school lasted 10 minutes. In addition to Brun, he killed one teacher and five students; 14 other students were wounded.

After Weise's death it was noted by relatives that he was being prescribed Prozac in increasing dosages. The news further inflamed the debate among doctors and scientists regarding the effects of antidepressants on children.

Weise submitted a number of different user profiles on the internet. Each provides a snapshot of a troubled youth. In one he lists *Elephant* and *Zero Day*, both inspired by the Columbine massacre, at the top of the list of his favourite films. His Yahoo! profile features the words of Hitler as his favourite quote. But of all these, it is Weise's MSN profile that is the most interesting and the most revealing. Instead of posting his own photograph, he provides a still from *Elephant* in which the two characters modelled on Columbine killers Eric Harris and Dylan Klebold, dressed in army fatigues, are entering the school where their massacre will take place.

Under 'A Little About Me', he writes, '16 years of accumulated rage suppressed by nothing more than brief glimpses of hope, which have all but faded to black. I can feel the urges within slipping through the cracks, the leash I can no longer hold...'

He follows this with his 'Favorite Things':

'moments where control becomes completely unattainable...

'times when maddened psycho paths [sic] briefly open the gates to hell, and let chaos flood through...

'those few individuals who care enough to reclaim their place...'

ADAM LANZA

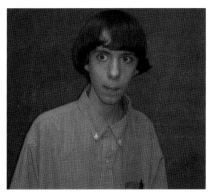

Many thought Lanza was harmless, but his obsession with school shootings kept growing

Newtown is a small sleepy town of 27,000 residents in Connecticut. It was the last place anyone would think of as the setting for a crime that would shock the world. On 14 December 2012, 20-year-old Adam Lanza changed everything. He shot his mother in the head before returning to his old school, Sandy Hook Elementary, in Newtown. Then, armed with a semi-automatic, military-style rifle, he burst into the school spraying bullets everywhere. Terrified teachers tried to calm their students as the nightmare unfolded. By the time the ordeal was over, Lanza's bullets had claimed the lives of 20 children, aged between 6 and 7, and six adults.

Adam Lanza lived most of his life in Newtown. To friends and neighbours, his parents Nancy and Peter appeared to be a loving, caring couple who did their best to provide their son with a good upbringing. But beneath the surface there were tensions.

In 2001 his parents separated. This was when things really started to turn sour. Lanza's relationship with his mother grew increasingly strained. Nancy was a gun enthusiast. She collected guns, kept them well stocked with ammunition and subscribed to a gun magazine. There were always lots of paper targets lying around the house. The family often went to the shooting range.

A disturbing family photo shows Adam Lanza as a toddler decked out in camouflage, wearing an ammunition belt and holding a gun to his mouth.

JEALOUSY

Lanza attended Sandy Hook Elementary School briefly as a child. His mother volunteered there between 1998 and 2012. This caused tension between them. He became jealous, believing that his mother showed more affection towards her students than she ever did towards him. By this time, he had moved on to Newtown High School. Though an honours student, he was taken

> A disturbing family photo shows Lanza as a toddler in camouflage, wearing an ammunition belt and holding a gun in his mouth

Adam Lanza pictured in 2005 when he would have been 12 or 13

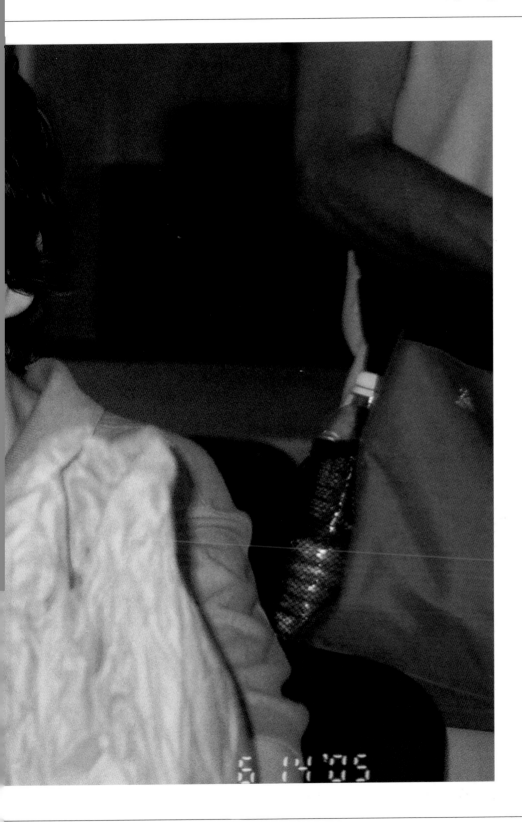

out of school to be home-schooled by his parents, and attended Western Connecticut State University in 2008 and 2009. Lanza had trouble socializing and making friends. He disliked anything that forced him into contact with other people – he hated birthdays, Christmas and holidays with a passion.

As a teenager he was diagnosed with Asperger syndrome. Lanza also suffered from obsessive compulsive disorder; he refused to touch doorknobs with his bare hands and changed his socks twenty times a day. He was prescribed drugs to help with his autism and other behavioural disorders but refused to take them. He grew increasingly angry at being forced to go for psychiatric tests at Yale. A nurse there, who saw him between 2006 and 2007, described him as 'emotionally paralyzed'.

In the fifth grade he wrote a story with another boy entitled 'The Big Book of Granny'. The story is about an old woman who kills people indiscriminately with the gun in her cane. In one chapter, there's a game called Hide and Go Die. In it, one character stated rather chillingly, 'I like hurting people... especially children.'

OBSESSED WITH MASS MURDER

Like many boys, Lanza was fascinated by conflict and guns. But it didn't stop there. He became obsessed by the mass shootings at Columbine High School in 1999 and at Northern Illinois University in 2008. The Newtown report, released in November 2013, noted he had 'hundreds of documents, images, videos pertaining to the Columbine H.S. massacre, including what appears to be a complete copy of the investigation'.

In his bedroom he kept a collection of newspaper cuttings on school shootings and there was a game called 'School Shooting' on his computer. On the wall was a huge spreadsheet featuring the top 500 mass murders of all time, which he had created himself, and he had also written a document listing the prerequisites for mass murder. But no one ever came into his room to find out what was going on.

> In his bedroom he kept a collection of newspaper cuttings on school shootings. On the wall was a huge spreadsheet of mass murders

Increasingly, Lanza began to cut himself off from the outside world. His mother may have been trying too hard to protect him. She didn't insist that he take the medication he had been prescribed. She also cancelled follow-up trips with mental health professionals. After 2008, he stopped having any treatment at all. Nancy Lanza struggled to accept the fact that her son had disabilities. She

Lanza became increasingly cut off and was clearly beginning to contemplate his own gun massacre

repeatedly described her son as 'gifted' when his intellectual abilities were really quite average.

As he grew older, his parents struggled to break through the barriers he put up. Despite living in the same house as his mother, he only contacted her by email. At one point, he didn't speak to her for three months. The windows of his room were covered with black garbage bags and he let no one else in. At the time of the killings, he hadn't seen his father for two years.

There was only one friend Lanza felt able to connect with. He remains anonymous and his testimony has only come out with the publication of the Sandy Hook Report. The two friends used to meet to play the video game *Dance Dance Revolution* and they talked about everything from Japanese techno music to paedophilia to chimp society. Lanza spent so much time playing *Dance Dance Revolution* that he acquired the nickname the 'DDR guy'.

In June 2012 the friends had a falling-out over a movie. Just months before the shooting, Lanza had thus lost his only buddy and became more and more isolated. He spent the three months before the shooting playing video games, studying previous mass murders and interacting online with a community of murder enthusiasts.

Lanza had developed his own theory of mass murder. As he saw it, they always occurred 'in contexts which involve some permutation of alienation'. His view of society was a gloomy one. He talked of the 'rape of civilization' and he railed against 'enculturing human children'. He put up post after post on online forums, explaining his philosophy, obsessing over mass killings and egging on others to bloodthirsty acts. No one ever intervened.

ANOREXIC

He was a scrawny teenager who suffered from anorexia. His eating habits were unhealthy. He would add salt to his drinking water. At the time of his death he was six feet tall but weighed only 112 pounds. In retrospect, the chief medical examiner suggested that malnutrition might have caused damage to his brain.

Nancy Lanza was only too aware that her son had a violent streak. Just a week before the shooting, she told a friend that she was afraid that he was getting worse. He kept burning himself with a lighter, but Nancy was afraid that he might try to commit suicide. Nancy had health issues herself. She had recently been diagnosed with MS.

On 10 December 2012 Nancy Lanza made a fateful decision which might have precipitated the killings. She decided to try an 'experiment'. She would leave Lanza on his own for a few days while she made a trip to New Hampshire. A few hours after she left, there were signs that her 'experiment' wasn't going too well. Adam had bumped his head and was bleeding.

Helped by the rescue services, a child escapes from the scene of the shootings

On the evening of 13 December, she returned home for the last time. At 9.00 a.m. the next day, Nancy Lanza was sleeping peacefully in her bed when her son entered and shot her in the head with her own gun. He took her guns, a Bushmaker XM15-E2S rifle, a civilian version of the semi-automatic weapon used by the US Army in Afghanistan and Iraq, and two handguns, a Glock pistol and a Sig Sauer, and left the house. Armed to the teeth, he climbed into his mother's car and drove to his old school, Sandy Hook Elementary.

The doors to the school were locked, so Lanza shot his way in through a nearby glass panel. Dressed in black clothing, sunglasses and a green utility vest, he struck a terrifying figure. The first shots fired were heard over the

Town volunteers of the Sandy Hook Fire and Rescue Department were some of the first people on the scene after the shooting. Here, they hug during a minute of silence held on 21 December 2012

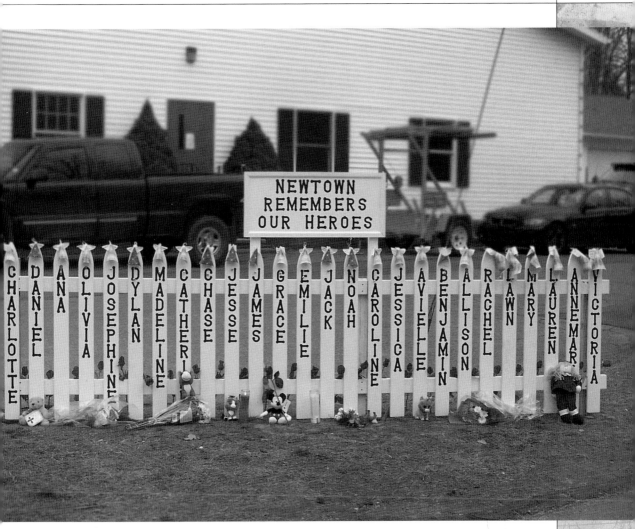

A touching picket fence memorial to the 26 victims, young and old, of Adam Lanza: Newtown will never be able to forget the terrible day that they were gunned down in cold blood

school intercom. The head janitor saw Lanza and yelled at him: 'Put the gun down!' Lanza ignored him and proceeded to kill the school's principal, Dawn Hochsprung, and the school psychologist, Mary Sherlach.

Lanza moved on to Lauren Rousseau's first-grade classroom. Rousseau had sent her children to the back of the room and was trying to hide them in a bathroom as Lanza entered. Soon Rousseau, Rachel D'Avino, a behavioural therapist, and 14 children were dead. A six-year-old girl was the only survivor of the attack. She managed to phone her mother: 'Mommy, I'm okay, but all my friends are dead.'

Kaitlin Roig-DeBellis hid her students in a tiny three-by-four-foot bathroom. She told them: 'If we're going to live, we have to find a hiding place … Evil is coming for us and there's nowhere to go.'

This spontaneous roadside shrine to those who died was erected at the school gates. It asks a question no one has yet answered...

Roig-DeBellis instructed her students to remain silent, and barricaded the door. One of them told her, 'I don't want to die before Christmas.' Eventually, the police arrived and knocked loudly. Terrified, she demanded some ID before she opened up. A badge slid under the door and she flung it open in relief.

Some teachers read stories to their children and others quietly sang Christmas carols. Twenty-seven-year-old Victoria Soto died shielding a child from Lanza's gunfire.

Yvonne Cech and Maryann Jacob hid their students in the library and pushed a filing cabinet against the door when they could not get the lock to work. Lanza tried to enter and, when it proved too much work, he moved on to easier prey.

It was only five minutes from the sound of the first gunshots to the welcome whine of police sirens, but it was already too late. Over one hundred rounds had already been fired. Police officers encountered a horrific scene. Bullet-ridden corpses of children and teachers alike were strewn across the school. Trauma teams were assembled ready to deal with any casualties and the emergency room of the nearest hospital was prepared to receive an influx of visitors. In the end only three victims reached the hospital. The others were already dead. The final shot was fired at 9:40 a.m. – it was Lanza taking his own life.

For the survivors, the memory of this terrible day never goes away. Kaitlin Roig-Debellis remembers it 'every second of every minute of every single day'. The community of Newtown, Connecticut, still struggles to come to terms with the horrific event.

One of the teacher's daughters still cannot believe it happened. According to Ashley Cech, 'If you know Newtown, if you know Sandy Hook, you just had this idea that nothing wrong could happen there.'

Sadly, Adam Lanza proved otherwise.

OMAR MATEEN

Before 12 June 2016, no one knew the name of Omar Mateen. Now he is infamous as the worst spree killer in recent US history.

Omar Mateen was born in New York on 16 November 1986 under the name Omar Mir Seddique. His parents were moderate Muslims who had immigrated to the United States from Afghanistan. According to their friends they were an 'all-American' family. He spent most of his childhood in the small Florida town of Port St. Lucie.

Mateen's ex-wife said that he was 'mentally unstable and mentally ill', yet he had a licence to work as a security guard and for 'concealed [gun] carry' in Florida. He also had a history of steroid abuse…

Mateen wtih his second wife Noor Zahi Salman and their three-year-old son. His first wife, Sitora, claimed that he had frequently beaten her and that her parents had had to come and rescue her from his clutches

His father Sedique Mateen was an outspoken Afghan activist who appeared in programmes on a satellite TV channel aimed at the Afghan immigrant community. He loved posing in military fatigues and putting himself forward as a suitable candidate to be Afghan president.

Friends and neighbours remember Omar Mateen as an angry and troubled child. At Mariposa Elementary, he began to show the signs of the propensity for violence that would characterize his life.

A third-grade teacher described him as 'verbally abusive, rude and aggressive' and in the seventh grade, he had to be transferred to a different class to stop him causing trouble. He bullied other children, particularly girls. Mateen struggled with school discipline and often required personal tutoring. His father did little to improve the situation, dismissing complaints against his son in a high-handed fashion and showing antagonism towards female teachers.

At high school, things got worse. At the age of 14, Mateen was expelled from Martin County High School after a fight in maths class, for which he was arrested. He moved on quickly to Spectrum, a high school for students with behavioural issues.

Fights and suspensions followed him throughout his high school career.

While most of the country reacted with shock and horror to the attacks of 11 September, Mateen applauded the terrorists. He even claimed that Osama bin Laden was his uncle and had taught him how to shoot AK-47s.

Life on the minimum wage

The first few years of his adult life were spent traipsing from one minimum-wage job to the next. He worked as a bagger at Publix, a cashier at Chik-fil-A and a sales associate at Hollister Clothing and General Nutrition Center (GNC).

But Mateen had aspirations. The chubby teenager was driven on by twin desires: to improve his physique, and to become a police officer. One was more easily achievable for someone like him. Working out constantly, with the help of certain chemical enhancements, the change in Mateen's body was obvious to everyone who knew him.

Mateen attended Indian River State College, earning a degree in criminal justice technology. He began working for the Florida Department of Corrections in 2006. Following the Virginia Tech shootings of April 2007, he started bringing a gun to class, resulting in his dismissal before he could qualify as a fully certified corrections officer.

Instead, he went to work for G4S, a British-based private security firm, but even there he could not keep himself out of trouble. His comments on terrorism – he claimed connections to Al-Qaeda – drew the FBI's attention.

He married an Uzbeki woman, Sitora Yusufiy, in 2008, but after four months they separated when she claimed physical and emotional abuse by her husband.

His second marriage, this time to Noor Zahi Salman, was more successful. They had a son. Mateen continued to live in South Florida as he had done for much of his life, residing at Fort Pierce, just 100 miles from Orlando.

Mateen was not a particularly devout Muslim. In fact, he chose to legally change his name from the traditional Afghan form 'Omar Mir Seddique', meaning 'Omar, son of Seddique', to something more American, Omar Mateen.

> **Mateen drank heavily and took drugs. He had once been greatly angered by the sight of two men kissing, but that may not tell the whole story**

He did occasionally attend the Islamic Center of Fort Pierce, where his three sisters were active volunteers. But he also drank heavily, took drugs and rarely talked about Islam with his friends. His wife Noor came from a more devout family than Mateen; she would fast for Ramadan and occasionally wore the hijab, but you could never call her a fundamentalist.

There was one thing above all that probably left Mateen conflicted. In the aftermath of the shootings, his father said his son had once been greatly angered by the sight of two men kissing, but that may not tell the whole story.

From his time at Indian River college, friends and colleagues began to wonder if Mateen was gay. He attended gay night clubs with friends and was a member of gay dating apps such as Grindr. For most of his life he showed no evidence of homophobia. His father, however, was not so tolerant, and would never have entertained the possibility that a son of his could be homosexual.

THE MASSACRE

Between the 5 and 9 June 2016, Mateen travelled to Orlando and visited Pulse nightclub several times. At this popular gay bar, Mateen would sit and drink in a corner by himself, though the owner of Pulse rejects any suggestion that Mateen was a regular customer.

Omar Mateen purchased a Glock 9mm handgun and a SIG Sauer MCX rifle. The latter was a semi-automatic rifle initially developed for the American special forces and then adapted for civilian use. His wife, Noor Salman, knew what was happening. After the attack she admitted to the FBI that she had accompanied him to Pulse nightclub on his earlier visits and had helped him to buy ammunition. On the Saturday evening of the massacre as he prepared to leave for Orlando, Salman warned him against doing anything crazy. But she made no attempt to call the police.

On 11 June, the evening of the killings, Mateen posted messages on the social networking platform Facebook confirming his allegiance to Islamic State:

Police and rescue officers monitor the scene outside Pulse in the aftermath of the shootings by lone wolf gunman Omar Mateen; many hardened lawmen were shocked at what had taken place the night before

Members of Orange County's Sheriff's Department and Florida State Highway Patrol show the strain of dealing with the gruesome results of Mateen's insane shooting spree

'I pledge my alliance to abu bakr al Baghdadi ... may Allah accept me ... The real muslims will never accept the filthy ways of the west. You kill innocent women and children by doing us airstrikes ... now taste the Islamic state vengeance.'

Just before he began his attack, Mateen called 911 and once more pledged his allegiance to ISIS. Equipped with two guns and with murder in his heart, he entered Pulse nightclub at 2:00 a.m. on 12 June 2016 and the shooting began. It was Latin Night; 320 patrons were happily drinking, dancing and enjoying the atmosphere.

A police officer was working overtime at the club and returned fire almost immediately, but was unable to prevent Mateen from killing his first victims. Mateen then opened fire on hundreds of innocent partiers inside the building. At first, some revellers mistook the sound of gunshots for music. But when the blood started flowing, reality set in.

In the dark a scene of horror and confusion was unfolding. At 2:09 a.m., a simple warning was posted on Pulse's Facebook page: 'Everyone get out of pulse and keep running.'

Soon social media was buzzing with news of the shooting as the terrified clubbers attempted to get the message out to friends and family, for example 'Omg. Shooting at pulse. We hid in the bathroom. And we can't find our friends' or 'Walking to Orlando Regional Medical Center now. I'm ok. Fred got shot. I've never seen so much blood and mayhem or been so scared ever.'

The victims were not the only ones attempting to communicate with loved ones. Omar Mateen asked his wife by text if she had 'seen the news'. She simply replied that she loved him.

Approximately 100 officers from the Orange County Sherriff's Office arrived, but by then Mateen had taken a number of hostages. Survivors overheard

The damaged rear wall of Pulse nightclub: a SWAT team crashed their armoured vehicle through the brickwork to put an end to the siege

Mateen claim that he wouldn't stop his assault until America stopped bombing 'his country'.

Police hostage negotiators spoke to Mateen by phone three times between 2:48 and 3:27 a.m. It was not until 5:53 a.m that the nightmare was over. By this time, SWAT team members had forcibly entered the building by crashing an armoured vehicle through the wall and Mateen had been killed in the ensuing shootout.

By the end of the night, 49 people were dead and another 53 injured. It was the worst mass shooting by an individual in United States history and the worst terrorist attack since 9/11.

The makeshift memorial outside Pulse nightclub, which became a shrine for people wanting to show their depth of feeling over the massacre. Pulse was slated to re-open in memory of the victims

BIBLIOGRAPHY

Frank W. Anderson, *The Dark Strangler*. Calgary: Frontier, 1974

Timothy Appleby, 'Angry Texans Want Guns, More Guns', *The Globe and Mail*, 11 December, 1993

Theo Arnoson, *Prince Eddy and the Homosexual Underworld*. London: John Murray, 1994

Jean Benedetti, *Gilles de Rais*. New York: Stein and Day, 1972

Mark Bourie, *By Reason of Inanity: The David Michael Krueger Story*. Toronto: Hounslow, 1997

Albert Borowitz, 'The History and Traditions of Fact-Based Crime Literature'. *Legal Studies Forum* 29:2, 2005

Brian Busby, *Character Parts: Who's Really Who in CanLit*. Toronto: Knopf Canada, 2003

Erland Clouston and Sarah Boseley, 'Dunblane Massacre'. *The Guardian*, 14 March 1996

Robert Cullen, *The Killer Department: Detective Victor Burakov's Eight-Year Hunt for the Most Savage Serial Killer in Russian History*. New York: Pantheon, 1993

Oliver Cyriax, *Crime: An Encyclopedia*. London: André Deutsch, 1993

Lionel Dahmer, *A Father's Story*. New York: Morrow, 1994

Monica Davey, 'Behind the Why of a Rampage, Loner With a Taste for Nazism', *The New York Times*, 23 March 2005

— and Gardiner Harris, 'Family Wonders if Prozac Prompted School Shootings', *The New York Times*, 23 March 2005

— and Jodi Wilgoren, 'Signs of Danger Were Missed in a Troubled Teenager's Life', *The New York Times*, 24 March 2005

Carol Anne Davis, *Women Who Kill: Profiles of Female Serial Killers*. London: Allison and Busby, 2001

Hugh Douglas, *Burke and Hare: The True Story*. London: Hale, 1973

Daniel Farson, *Jack the Ripper*. London: Sphere, 1973

'"Female Vipers" Cited in Letter to Sisters', *The Globe and Mail*, 18 October 1991

Jon Ferry, *The Olson Murders*. Toronto: Cameo, 1982

George Fetherling, *A Biographical Dictionary of the World's Assassins*. Toronto: Random House Canada, 2001

Joseph C. Fisher, *Killer Among Us: Public Reactions to Serial Murder*. Westport, Connecticut: Praeger, 1997

James Alan Fox and Jack Levin, *Extreme Killing: Understanding Serial and Mass Murder*. Thousand Oaks, California: Sage, 2005

Daniel Francis, *Red Light Neon: A History of Vancouver's Sex Trade*. Vancouver: Subway, 2006

David Franke, *The Torture Doctor*. New York: Hawthorne, 1975

Nancy Gibbs and Timothy Roche, 'The Columbine Tapes', *Time*, 20 December 1999

Mel Gordon, *Voluptuous Panic: The Erotic World of Weimar Berlin*. Venice, California: Feral House, 2000

John Gray, 'A Case of Mind Over Murder', *The Globe and Mail*, 22 August 1992

Peter Haining, *Sweeney Todd: The Real Story of the Demon Barber of Fleet Street*. London: Boxtree, 1993

'He Murdered Women', *The Globe* (Toronto), 29 June 1892

Eric W. Hickey, *Serial Murderers and Their Victims*. Pacific Grove, California: Brooks/Cole, 1991

'Holmes Hanged', *The Globe and Mail*, 8 May 1896

W. Leslie Holmes, *Where Shadows Linger: The Untold story of the RCMP's Olson Murder Investigation*. Victoria: Heritage House, 2000

'I Do Rotten, Horrible Things', *Time*, 8 January 1979

Greg Johnson, *Invisible Writer: A Biography of Joyce Carol Oates*. New York: Dutton, 1998

Kirk Johnson, 'Survivors of High School Rampage Left With Injuries and Many Questions', *The New York Times*, 25 March 2005

Sebastian Junger, *A Death in Belmont*. New York: Norton, 2006

Susan Kelly, *The Boston Stranglers: The Public Conviction of Albert DeSalvo and the True Story of Eleven Shocking Murders*. New York: Birch Lane, 1995

Alix Krista, '"I Thought – I'm in Serious Trouble Here"', *The Guardian*, 14 December 2006

Erik Larson, *The Devil in the White City: Murder, Magic, and Madness at the Fair that Changed America*. New York: Crown, 2003

'Last 9 Gacy Victims, Still Unidentified, Are Buried', *The New York Times*, 14 June 1981

Elliott Leyton, *Hunting Humans: The Rise of the Modern Multiple Murderer*. Toronto: McClelland and Stewart, 1986

— *Men of Blood: Murder in Everyday Life*. Toronto: McClelland and Stewart, 1996

Victor Malarek, 'Killer Fraternized with Men in Army Fatigues', *The Globe and Mail*, 9 September 1989

'Mass Killer Twice Held, Freed', *The Globe and Mail*, 18 April 1992

Jason Moss with Jeffrey Kottler, *The Last Victim: A True-Life Journey into the Mind of the Serial Killer*. New York: Warner, 1999

Ian Mulgrew, *Final Payoff: The True Price of Convicting Clifford Robert Olson*. Toronto: Seal, 1990

Bill O'Brien, *Agents of Mayhem: The Global Phenomenon of Mass Murder*. Auckland. New Zealand: David Bateman, 2000

'Officers Tell Jury of Letting Dahmer Keep Boy', *The New York Times*, 13 February 1992

Maureen Orth, *Vulgar Favours: Andrew Cunanan, Gianni Versace, and the Largest Failed Manhunt in U.S. History*. New York: Delacorte, 1999

Rank Rich, 'Loving Jeffrey Dahmer', *The New York Times*, 17 March 1994

Scott Rothchild, 'Texas Gunman Kills 22 People in Restaurant', *The Globe and Mail*, 17 October 1991

Lyle Saxon, Edward Dreyer and Robert Tallant, *Gumbo Ya Ya: A Collection of Louisiana Folk Tales*. Boston: Houghton Mifflin, 1945

Harold Schechter, Bestial: *The Savage Trail of a True American Monster*. New York: Pocket, 1999

— *Depraved: The Shocking True Story of America's First Serial Killer*. New York: Pocket, 1994

— *The Serial Killer Files*. New York: Ballantine, 2003

'Shooting Rampage at Killeen Luby's Left 24 Dead', *The Houston Chronicle*, 10 August 2001

Gini Sikes, 'Such a Nice Young Man', *Mirabella*, 3:69. April 1992

'Texas Police Were Warned about Gunman, Women Say', *The Globe and Mail*, 18 October 1991

Donald Thomas, *The Victorian Underworld*. London: John Murray, 1998

Tony Thorne, *Countess Dracula: The Life and Times of the Bloody Countess, Elisabeth Báthory*. London: Bloomsbury, 1997

Colin Wilson, *The Serial Killers: A Study in the Psychology of Violence*. London: Allen, 1990

— and Robin Odell, *Jack the Ripper: Summing Up and Verdict*. London: Bantam, 1987

Leonard Wolf, *Bluebeard: The Life and Times of Gilles de Rais*. New York: Potter, 1980

Morris Wolfe, *Essays, New and Selected*. Toronto: grubstreet, n.d

INDEX

Index/Picture Credits

PICTURE CREDITS

AKG: 67

Barrington Barber: 31, 33, 47, 55, 58, 59, 62, 83, 113

Corbis: 7, 14, 28, 36, 37, 52, 53, 73, 84, 90, 93, 95, 97, 99, 103, 105, 108, 109, 110, 125, 126, 128, 134, 142, 143, 144, 145, 147, 151, 153, 156, 159, 162, 167, 168, 170, 181, 182, 183, 186, 188, 189

Dore: 30, 41

Getty: 16 (b), 24, 115, 116, 118, 1210 (t), 133, 138, 139, 150, 161, 175, 176, 192-3, 196 (x2), 204 (t)

Kobal: 39, 65, 78

Mary Evans: 13, 15, 25, 40

PA: 8, 136, 164, 184, 199

Rex: 66, 70

Shutterstock: 16 (t), 64, 72 (b), 75, 87, 106, 107, 119 (x2 – Joseph Solum), 120 (b – Vicki L. Miller), 121, 130, 160, 166, 195, 197, 198, 202, 203, 204 (b)

Topfoto: 17, 21, 43, 77, 80 (t), 131

'Vescojr': 18; **Hsin Ho**: 19; **Timo Newton-Syms**: 22; **Kevin Turpeinen**: 114; **Jennifer Graevell**: 141

We have made every attempt to contact the copyright-owners of the photographs and illustrations within this book. Any oversights or omissions will be corrected in future editions.